5294 HC 75

BARRIE PRICE & JEAN-LOUIS ARBEY

BUGATTI

THE 8-CYLINDER TOURING CARS 1920-1934
TYPES 28, 30, 38, 38a, 44 & 49

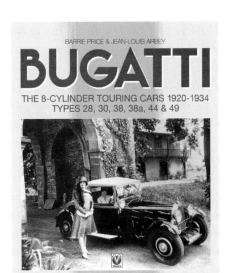

OTHER GREAT VELOCE BOOKS!

SpeedPro Series
4-Cylinder Engine – How to Blueprint & Build a Short Block for High Performance (Hammill)
Alfa Romeo DOHC High-Performance Manual (Kartalamakis)
Alfa Romeo V6 Engine High-Perfomance Manual (Kartalamakis)
BMC 998cc A-Series Engine – How to Power Tune (Hammill)
1275cc A-Series High-Performance Manual (Hammill)
Camshafts – How to Choose & Time them for Maximum Power (Hammill)
Cylinder Heads – How to Build, Modify & Power Tune Updated & Revised Edition (Burgess & Gollan)
Distributor-type Ignition Systems – How to Build & Power Tune (Hammill)
Fast Road Car – How to Plan and Build Revised & Updated Colour New Edition (Stapleton)
Ford SOHC 'Pinto' & Sierra Cosworth DOHC Engines – How to Power Tune Updated & Enlarged Edition (Hammill)
Ford V8 – How to Power Tune Small Block Engines (Hammill)
Harley-Davidson Evolution Engines – How to Build & Power Tune (Hammill)
Holley Carburetors – How to Build & Power Tune Revised & Updated Edition (Hammill)
Jaguar XK Engines – How to Power Tune Revised & Updated Colour Edition (Hammill)
MG Midget & Austin-Healey Sprite – How to Power Tune Updated & Revised Edition (Stapleton)
MGB 4-Cylinder Engine – How to Power Tune (Burgess)
MGB V8 Power – How to Give Your, Third Colour Edition (Williams)
MGB, MGC & MGB V8 – How to Improve (Williams)
Mini Engines – How to Power Tune on a Small Budget Colour Edition (Hammill)
Motorsport – Getting Started (Collins)
Nitrous Oxide High-Performance Manual (Langfield)
Rover V8 Engines – How to Power Tune (Hammill)
Sportscar/Kitcar Suspension & Brakes – How to Build & Modify Enlarged & Updated 2nd Edition (Hammill)
SU Carburettor High-Performance Manual (Hammill)
Suzuki 4x4 – How to Modify for Serious Off-Road Action (Richardson)
Tiger Avon Sportscar – How to Build Your Own Updated & Revised 2nd Edition (Dudley)
TR2, 3 & TR4 – How to Improve (Williams)
TR5, 250 & TR6 – How to Improve (Williams)
TR7 & TR8, How to Improve (Williams)
V8 Engine – How to Build a Short Block for High Performance (Hammill)
Volkswagen Beetle Suspension, Brakes & Chassis – How to Modify for High Performance (Hale)
Volkswagen Bus Suspension, Brakes & Chassis – How to Modify for High Performance (Hale)
Weber DCOE, & Dellorto DHLA Carburetors – How to Build & Power Tune 3rd Edition (Hammill)

Those were the days ... Series
Alpine Trials & Rallies 1910-1973 (Pfundner)
Austerity Motoring (Bobbitt)
Brighton National Speed Trials (Gardiner)
British Police Cars (Walker)
Crystal Palace by (Collins)
Dune Buggy Phenomenon (Hale)
Dune Buggy Phenomenon Volume 2 (Hale)
MG's Abingdon Factory (Moylan)
Motor Racing at Brands Hatch in the Seventies (Parker)
Motor Racing at Goodwood in the Sixties (Gardiner)
Motor Racing at Oulton Park in the 1960s (McFadyen)
Three Wheelers (Bobbitt)

Enthusiast's Restoration Manual Series
Citroën 2CV, How to Restore (Porter)
Classic Car Bodywork, How to Restore (Thaddeus)
Classic Car Electrics (Thaddeus)
Classic Cars, How to Paint (Thaddeus)
Reliant Regal, How to Restore (Payne)
Triumph TR2/3/3A, How to Restore (Williams)
Triumph TR4/4A, How to Restore (Williams)
Triumph TR5/250 & 6, How to Restore (Williams)
Triumph TR7/8, How to Restore (Williams)
Volkswagen Beetle, How to Restore (Tyler)
Yamaha FS1-E, How to Restore (Watts)

Essential Buyer's Guide Series
Alfa GT (Booker)
Alfa Romeo Spider Giulia (Booker)
BMW GS (Henshaw)
Citroën 2CV (Paxton)
Jaguar E-type 3.8 & 4.2-litre (Crespin)
Jaguar E-type V12 5.3-litre (Crespin)
Jaguar/Daimler XJ6, XJ12 & Sovereign (Crespin)
MGB & MGB GT (Williams)
Mercedes-Benz 280SL-560SL Roadsters (Bass)
Mercedes-Benz 'Pagoda' 230SL, 250SL & 280SL Roadsters & Coupés (Bass)
Morris Minor (Newell)

Porsche 928 (Hemmings)
Rolls-Royce Silver Shadow & Bentley T-Series (Bobbitt)
Triumph Bonneville (Henshaw)
Triumph TR6 (Williams)
VW Beetle (Cservenka & Copping)
VW Bus (Cservenka & Copping)

Auto-Graphics Series
Fiat-based Abarths (Sparrow)
Jaguar Mkl & II Saloons (Sparrow)
Lambretta LI series scooters (Sparrow)

Rally Giants Series
Big Healey – 100-Six & 3000 (Robson)
Ford Escort Mkl (Robson)
Lancia Stratos (Robson)
Peugeot 205 T16 (Robson)
Subaru Impreza (Robson)

General
1½-litre GP Racing 1961-1965 (Whitelock)
AC Two-litre Saloons & Buckland Sportscars (Archibald)
Alfa Romeo Giulia Coupé GT & GTA (Tipler)
Alfa Tipo 33 (McDonough & Collins)
Anatomy of the Works Minis (Moylan)
Armstrong-Siddeley (Smith)
Autodrome (Collins & Ireland)
Automotive A-Z, Lane's Dictionary of Automotive Terms (Lane)
Automotive Mascots (Kay & Springate)
Bahamas Speed Weeks, The (O'Neil)
Bentley Continental, Corniche and Azure (Bennett)
Bentley MkVI, Rolls-Royce Silver Wraith, Dawn & Cloud/ Bentley R & S-series (Nutland)
BMC Competitions Department Secrets (Turner, Chambers Browning)
BMW 5-Series (Cranswick)
BMW Z-Cars (Taylor)
British 250cc Racing Motorcycles by Chris Pereira
British Cars, The Complete Catalogue of, 1895-1975 (Culshaw & Horrobin)
BRM – a mechanic's tale (Salmon)
BRM V16 (Ludvigsen)
Bugatti Type 40 (Price & Arbey)
Bugatti T44 & T49 (Price & Arbey)
Bugatti 46/50 Updated Edition (Price)
Bugatti 57 2nd Edition (Price)
Caravans, The Illustrated History 1919-1959 (Jenkinson)
Caravans, The Illustrated History from 1960 (Jenkinson)
Chrysler 300 – America's Most Powerful Car 2nd Edition (Ackerson)
Chrysler PT Cruiser (Ackerson)
Citroën DS (Bobbitt)
Cobra – The Real Thing! (Legate)
Cortina – Ford's Bestseller (Robson)
Coventry Climax Racing Engines (Hammill)
Daimler SP250 New Edition (Long)
Datsun Fairlady Roadster to 280ZX – The Z-car Story (Long)
Dino – The V6 Ferrari (Long)
Dodge Dynamite! (Grist)
Drive on the Wild Side, A – 20 extreme driving adventures from around the world (Weaver)
Ducati 750 Bible, The (Falloon)
Dune Buggy, Building a – The Essential Manual (Shakespeare)
Dune Buggy Files (Hale)
Dune Buggy Handbook (Hale)
Edward Turner: the man behind the motorcycles (Clew)
Fiat & Abarth 124 Spider & Coupé (Tipler)
Fiat & Abarth 500 & 600 2nd edition (Bobbitt)
Fiats, Great Small (Ward)
Ford F100/F150 Pick-up 1948-1996 (Ackerson)
Ford F150 1997-2005 (Ackerson)
Ford GT – Then, and Now (Streather)
Ford GT40 (Legate)
Ford in Miniature (Olson)
Ford Model Y (Roberts)
Ford Thunderbird from 1954, The Book of the (Long)
Funky Mopeds (Skelton)
GT – The World's Best GT Cars 1953-73 (Dawson)
Hillclimbing & sprinting – The essential manual (Short)
Honda NSX (Long)
Jaguar, The Rise of (Price)
Jaguar XJ-S (Long)
Jeep CJ (Ackerson)
Jeep Wrangler (Ackerson)
Karmann-Ghia Coupé & Convertible (Bobbitt)
Lambretta Bible, The (Davies)
Lancia 037 (Collins)
Lancia Delta HF Integrale (Blaettel & Wagner)
Land Rover, The Half-Ton Military (Cook)
Laverda Twins & Triples Bible 1968-1986 (Falloon)
Lea-Francis Story, The (Price)
Lexus Story, The (Long)
little book of smart, The (Jackson)
Lola – The Illustrated History (1957-1977) (Starkey)

Lola – All the Sports Racing & Single-Seater Racing Cars 1978-1997 (Starkey)
Lola T70 – The Racing History & Individual Chassis Record 3rd Edition (Starkey)
Lotus 49 (Oliver)
MarketingMobiles, The Wonderful Wacky World of (Hale)
Mazda MX-5/Miata 1.6 Enthusiast's Workshop Manual (Grainger & Shoemark)
Mazda MX-5/Miata 1.8 Enthusiast's Workshop Manual (Grainger & Shoemark)
Mazda MX-5 Miata: the book of the world's favourite sportscar (Long)
Mazda MX-5 Miata Roadster (Long)
MGA (Price Williams)
MGB & MGB GT – Expert Guide (Auto-Doc Series) (Williams)
MGB Electrical Systems (Astley)
Micro Caravans (Jenkinson)
Microcars at large! (Quellin)
Mini Cooper – The Real Thing! (Tipler)
Mitsubishi Lancer Evo, the road car & WRC story (Long)
Montlhéry, the story of the Paris autodrome (Boddy)
Morris Minor, 60 years on the road (Newell)
Moto Guzzi Sport & Le Mans Bible (Falloon)
Motor Movies – The Posters! (Veysey)
Motor Racing – Reflections of a Lost Era (Carter)
Motorcycle Road & Racing Chassis Designs (Knoakes)
Motorhomes, The Illustrated History (Jenkinson)
Motorsport in colour, 1950s (Wainwright)
Nissan 300ZX & 350Z – The Z-Car Story (Long)
Pass the Theory and Practical Driving Tests (Gibson & Hoole)
Peking to Paris 2007 (Young)
Plastic Toy Cars of the 1950s & 1960s (Ralston)
Pontiac Firebird (Cranswick)
Porsche Boxster (Long)
Porsche 356 (2nd edition) (Long)
Porsche 911 Carrera – The Last of the Evolution (Corlett)
Porsche 911R, RS & RSR, 4th Edition (Starkey)
Porsche 911 – The Definitive History 1963-1971 (Long)
Porsche 911 – The Definitive History 1971-1977 (Long)
Porsche 911 – The Definitive History 1977-1987 (Long)
Porsche 911 – The Definitive History 1987-1997 (Long)
Porsche 911 – The Definitive History 1997-2004 (Long)
Porsche 911SC 'Super Carrera' – The Essential Companion (Streather)
Porsche 914 & 914-6: The Definitive History Of The Road & Competition Cars (Long)
Porsche 924 (Long)
Porsche 944 (Long)
Porsche 993 'King of Porsche' – The Essential Companion (Streather)
Porsche Racing Cars – 1953 to 1975 (Long)
Porsche Racing Cars – 1976 on (Long)
Porsche – The Rally Story (Meredith)
Porsche: Three Generations of Genius (Meredith)
RAC Rally Action! (Gardiner)
Rallye Sport Fords: the inside story (Moreton)
Redman, Jim – 6 Times World Motorcycle Champion: The Autobiography (Redman)
Rolls-Royce Silver Shadow/Bentley T Series Corniche & Camargue Revised & Enlarged Edition (Bobbitt)
Rolls-Royce Silver Spirit, Silver Spur & Bentley Mulsanne 2nd Edition (Bobbitt)
RX-7 – Mazda's Rotary Engine Sportscar (updated & revised new edition) (Long)
Scooters & Microcars, The A-Z of popular (Dan)
Singer Story: Cars, Commercial Vehicles, Bicycles & Motorcycles (Atkinson)
SM – Citroën's Maserati-engined Supercar (Long & Claverol)
Subaru Impreza: the road car and WRC story (Long)
Taxi! The Story of the 'London' Taxicab (Bobbitt)
Toyota Celica & Supra, The book of Toyota's Sports Coupés (Long)
Toyota MR2 Coupés & Spyders (Long)
Triumph Motorcycles & the Meriden Factory (Hancox)
Triumph Speed Twin & Thunderbird Bible (Woolridge)
Triumph Tiger Cub Bible (Estall)
Triumph Trophy Bible (Woolridge)
Triumph TR6 (Kimberley)
Unraced (Collins)
Velocette Motorcycles – MSS to Thruxton Updated & Revised (Burris)
Virgil Exner – Visioneer: The official biography of Virgil M Exner designer extraordinaire (Grist)
Volkswagen Bus Book, The (Bobbitt)
Volkswagen Bus or Van to Camper, How to Convert (Porter)
Volkswagens of the World (Glen)
VW Beetle Cabriolet (Bobbitt)
VW Beetle – The Car of the 20th Century (Copping)
VW Bus – 40 years of Splitties, Bays & Wedges (Copping)
VW Bus Book, The (Bobbitt)
VW Golf: five generations of fun (Copping & Cservenka)
VW – The air-cooled era (Copping)
VW T5 Camper Conversion Manual (Porter)
VW Campers (Copping)
Works Minis, The Last (Purves & Brenchley)
Works Rally Mechanic (Moylan)

WWW.VELOCE.CO.UK

First published in August 2007 by Veloce Publishing Limited, 33 Trinity Street, Dorchester DT1 1TT, England. Fax 01305 268864/e-mail info@veloce.co.uk/web www.veloce.co.uk or www.velocebooks.com.
ISBN: 978-1-901295-95-5/UPC: 6-36847-00195-7

BARRIE PRICE & JEAN-LOUIS ARBEY

BUGATTI

THE 8-CYLINDER TOURING CARS 1920-1934
TYPES 28, 30, 38, 38a, 44 & 49

VELOCE PUBLISHING
THE PUBLISHER OF FINE AUTOMOTIVE BOOKS

CONTENTS

INTRODUCTION

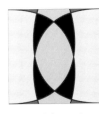During the 1914-18 war, Ettore Bugatti must have thought long and hard about his company's post-war policy. This would have been difficult to anticipate, of course, for it was not possible until near the end to foresee either the outcome of the war, or just how impoverished Western Europe would become. Bugatti had achieved a dominant position as a producer of high-performance small cars in a very short time. The market for expensive large and fast cars was known to be at the forefront of his mind, however, and a handful of experimental 5-litre machines had been built prior to the war. These had achieved a good measure of publicity by way of sporting success. We also know from surviving correspondence that Bugatti cherished the notion of one day building the ultimate car for the luxury market, which resulted in the stupendous Royale.

Although ostensibly a commercial disaster, when viewed some seventy-five years later, we are grateful for his indulgence. Certainly the world of motor cars is richer as a result of the production of these six 'super cars'.

We know that Bugatti's methods of manufacture and design were highly efficient; simple components and a great deal of interchangeability always remained his policy. The prestige accorded the Royale was out of all proportion to the number built, while the engineering of this car resulted in some savings when it came to the design of the later, and much more successful, Type 46.

The engine production costs of the Royale (Type 41) were later fully recouped by way of the Autorail business.

Bugatti soon made a sensible decision to mount a serious assault on the market for medium-sized touring cars with high performance and outstanding quality, which culminated in the Type 44 and the Type 49 series with which we are here concerned.

The small pre-war car, originally 13/27cc, later enlarged to 1500cc (Type 13 and derivatives) continued in production until 1926 and proved to be the mainstay for the firm, with a record production run for any Bugatti Type of about 2200 cars.

Ettore became converted to the 3-valve layout, initially seen in the 1912 5-litre car and in the wartime 16-cylinder aero-engine, which was still under development after many problems when the armistice was declared.

The straight-eight engine configuration also seems to have become a fixation with him, (the aero-engine consisted of 2 banks of vertical eights). In this regard Ettore was almost a pioneer and it was not until some years later that both US and European manufacturers took to this style with a vengeance. A great many makers, seduced by the apparent sales appeal and long bonnets of the straight-eight engined car, brought out models so fitted. The European versions almost all resulted in commercial failures, with disappointing performance and unexpected roughness, and many had poor induction systems resulting in flat spots and heavy fuel consumption. The straight-eight craze in Europe produced many disappointed customers, and by 1931 it was all over.

Although of little relevance to this story, the first car in which the author remembers travelling was a Hillman

Type 38 engine in a 35A racing car; 130 of this 'course imitation' car were made in the years 1926-1929. Chassis 4789 – motor 100A.

Moteur de type 38 utilisé dans une voiture de course de type 35A. 130 exemplaires ont été produits de 1926 a 1929. Chassis 4789; moteur 100A.

straight-eight which evokes obscure memories of a run from Coventry to Bournemouth for the annual holiday. Even the lowly Clyno concern built an experimental straight-eight which was discovered by a surprised official receiver when checking the firm's inventory.

American manufacturers were much more successful; primarily due to larger budgets for development, but also because American customers were generally satisfied with large, slow running and low compression engines.

For Bugatti, the basic problem with the straight-eight concerned the excessive length of the crankshaft, resulting in severe torsional vibration problems which proved difficult to tame to the point of acceptability. Ettore encountered the most appalling problems of roughness and vibration with his early 8-cylinder production cars, but persevered and

achieved a very good result by the time of the introduction of the 3-litre Type 44 when the straight-eight craze took hold, and so stole a march on his competitors.

ACKNOWLEDGEMENTS

The authors are grateful for the assistance of:
Terry Cardy, Jean-Michel Cérède, Denis Chourré, Lionel Decrey, Jean Feray, Pierre Foucheyrand, Benoit Grossier, Roland Jordi, Pierre-Yves Laugier, Lester Matthews, Hans Matti, Jean Novo, Gilles Pautu, Daniel Philippe, René Potet, The Lord Raglan, Royal Motor-Union de Liège, Laurent Rondoni, Norbert Steinhauser, Claude Taconetti, Nicolas Tellier, Jacques Thurel, Bruno Vendiesse, Michael Wood.

CHAPTER ONE

TYPE 44 DEVELOPMENT

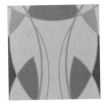 Bugatti had actually built a straight-eight, which consisted of 2 Type 13 engines coupled together, in 1914, but this could not have been very sensible. 1920-21 saw the design and construction of a 3-litre prototype with the design number Type 28. This car was of advanced specification, and featured a 9-bearing crankshaft with a vertical shaft in the middle of the engine to drive the overhead camshaft. Two cylinder blocks were employed, surmounted by one long cambox. This car also revealed the beginning of another Bugatti hallmark, in the form of the narrow, squared-off engine, milled all over to produce a unique and pleasing appearance that typified the tidy mind and thinking of this gifted individual. This car bore the unusual but not unknown feature of a gearbox located in the rear axle. The passengers would certainly be better insulated from the noise emitted by the gears of that period, and there would be less bulk to accommodate, which often interfered with the floor in the front compartment. The torque multiplication in bottom gear would not have loaded the propshaft, which was possibly the biggest advantage since universal joint couplings were troublesome in those early days. The disadvantages concerned a large increase in un-sprung weight, a complicated gear change linkage and, although the propshaft was relieved of much of the stress, it had to accelerate and decelerate with each change of gear.

The chassis was similar in layout to the small car but with an increase in length. The radiator, although of Bugatti style, differed from any other type.

The one car built, originally fitted with a Fiacre body of typical Bugatti style, was used for tests and appraisal. The body was removed but, miraculously, the chassis survived, together with various other experimental cars, in an outbuilding at the Molsheim works. The chassis, fitted with a recent body, now resides in the Schlumpf Museum at Mulhouse.

We can only conclude that business with the Brescia Types occupied all production facilities at the works, which was only just beginning to expand in size and facilities. Thus the Type 28 was abandoned.

The first production straight-eight engine was a 2-litre variant, designated Type 30, which followed standard Brescia Types 22 or 23 layout in all respects save the engine. This new power plant specified a bore and stroke of 60mm x 88mm respectively. The crankshaft ran in 3 main bearings, while big end lubrication relied on the standard Bugatti practice of jet feed from the crankcase wall, feeding into grooves in the circular web crankshaft and angled drillings to the big end journals.

The crankshaft of the Type 30 was carried on ball/roller races with a crank journal diameter of 65mm.

Bugatti adopted as standard a diameter of 45mm for big end bearings on Types 28, 30, 35A, 37, 38, 38A, 40, 40A, 44, 49 and even the 57, while the white metalled main bearings of Types 28, 37, 40, 40A, 44 and 49 were all settled at 50mm. This latter size was larger than most other makers adopted in the vintage period, and was particularly robust for the 1½-litre Types 37, 40 and 40A and, combined with a 5 bearing layout, contributed to the smooth running and ample safety margin of these 4-cylinder models.

By way of comparison, the Meadows 4ED 1½-litre engine of the same period, which found favour with British manufacturers, including Lea Francis and Frazer-Nash, sufficed with a main and big-end diameter of 1⅝in (41mm), while Alvis specified 50mm and 45mm respectively for main and big ends for its 12/50, both direct competitors with the Type 40 on the British market.

The Type 30, although abominably rough and fragile if driven fast, nevertheless found a market, and some 600 examples were built. Production of this car began in 1922, with first deliveries commencing in November of that year and giving way to the Type 38 in early 1926.

The Type 38 was given the definitive Bugatti front axle layout, first seen on the Type 35 racing car in 1924. The salient and unique feature of the design concerned the circular front axle beam which was polished all over, and employed boxes through which the front springs passed, secured by taper wedges. The rear of the front springs ran in sliding trunnions, which also became a feature of all models prior to the Type 57. It is strange to relate that the Type 38 continued with the fragile three-bearing engine of the 30, although guarantee complaints and general customer dissatisfaction must have become manifest. The first Type 38s were delivered in March 1926, while the final car was delivered in 1928, by which time 387 cars had been built. In order to boost the performance of the 2-litre Type 38, a supercharger was added, and the car became known as the Type 38A. The unit chosen was from the 1½-litre T39 racing car and so would have provided a modest boost. This modification would have added further load to the delicate crankshaft and bearing system, although the better gas distribution afforded by the supercharger may well have provided a smoother running unit. The final batch of approximately 50 cars was so fitted.

A most important change concerned the arrangement of the firing order – 1, 5, 2, 6, 3, 7, 4, 8 – specified for the touring models and also the roller bearing racing cars, Types 35, 39 and 51. The nine-bearing Type 44 commenced with 1, 5, 2, 6, 4, 8, 3, 7 but soon changed to 1, 6, 2, 5, 8, 3, 7, 4 resulting in a smoother engine, an order which remained for all 8-cylinder cars to the end of car production. Oil pump and drive modifications were carried out at approximately chassis number 44292.

Chassis frames for various touring types during the period 1921-28 show continual development. The experimental Type 28 design was simple in the extreme, with straight side rails in plan view forged from 4.5mm gauge high tensile steel. A noteworthy feature was the incredibly refined and tapered section leading to the front dumb irons. No other maker risked such a tiny section, and yet no car (in

the author's experience) has ever revealed stress cracks or failures in this vicinity; the stress at this point is very low, a factor appreciated by Bugatti. This feature was to be seen in all subsequent cars until the end of production in 1939.

120mm was specified as the depth from a point near the rear engine mount to where the rail 'kicks-up' to clear the rear axle. The final section ended in the boss which carried the rear spring, and the cross tube carried a depth of 85mm. The intention was to build 3 chassis lengths for the stillborn Type 28, varying by 600mm. The long chassis would have been a borderline case for acceptable stiffness, but in any case was never built.

The Type 30 frame followed the contemporary Brescia 4-cylinder cars which featured side rails which widened from a point near the rear engine mounting. This was in order to give a wider rear spring base and a better chance for the coachbuilders by way of support nearer to or directly below the body sides.

The gauge was now 6mm with a section depth of 94mm for a wheelbase of 2.55 metres (short) and 2.85 (long). The Type 38 we believe was only available in one wheelbase, 3.12 metres, and followed the Type 30 design except for an increase in chassis width of 12mm, and the maximum section depth returned to 120mm with a gauge now of 5mm.

The Type 44, which is the principal subject of this book and one of the most successful of all Bugattis (exceeded in production numbers only by the Brescia range), comprised the Type 38 chassis but with minor differences around the rear engine mount position.

This new car consisted of the original Type 28 engine but fitted with a Bugatti-designed crankshaft damper. The capacity was settled at three litres (69 x 100 bore and stroke).

A survey of the chassis parts schedule indicates that the main components of the chassis were of Type 30 origin, with the exception of the front axle and certain other details which were carried over from the Type 38.

The first car was completed in October 1927, while the final example apparently left the works in November 1930, during which period approximately 1100 chassis had been completed. This car was well received by the motoring press and proved a serious competitor in the marketplace of the time, capable of carrying 4 people at a maximum speed of 80mph with full saloon coachwork and in a high degree of comfort. Steering and roadholding were up to traditional Bugatti standards which, at the time and for many years, were second to none.

The final manifestation of this family was titled Type 49 and was similar in almost all respects except for an increase in cylinder bore of 3mm to 72mm and thus a capacity of 3.3 litres. The increase in size, presumably to maintain the performance of the T44 because coachwork was becoming heavier, and accessories, such as bumpers front and rear, also carried a weight penalty. One innovation concerned the fitting of two spark plugs per cylinder, and thus a 16-cylinder distributor. This necessitated a special scintilla switch incorporating 3 positions, for separate sets of plugs and all sixteen together. The second plug will have resulted in even less space for water around the cylinder head chamber, although no ill effects were noted. It is difficult, however, to envisage any advantage from this system save that of reliability in the event of a plug failure. The Type 49 chassis frame drawings cannot be found, probably because Type 44 frames were used, altered only in detail, such as shock absorber mounting points, and a change from friction

to hydraulic (Houdaille) dampers (rear only). The first car left the works in October 1930 and production continued until 1934, the last few cars being built in parallel with the first of the Type 57s. A total of approximately 480 cars were completed. Production was, therefore, running at approximately half that of the preceding model, clearly reflecting the difficult economic climate of the early '30s. Few specification changes occurred during the production life of the Type 49 although the previous oil filled clutch gave way to dry linings, while elegant cast aluminium wheels were optional features and most cars were so fitted. The 72mm bore was also specified for the short-lived Type 40A, although only with single plugs.

By Barrie Price

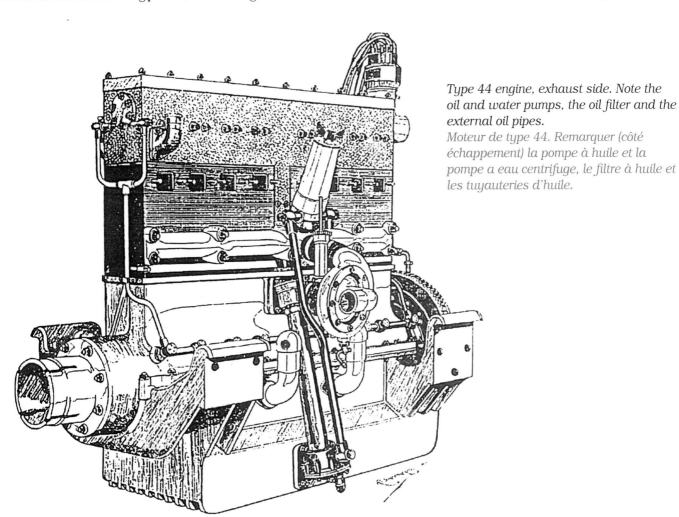

Type 44 engine, exhaust side. Note the oil and water pumps, the oil filter and the external oil pipes.

Moteur de type 44. Remarquer (côté échappement) la pompe à huile et la pompe a eau centrifuge, le filtre à huile et les tuyauteries d'huile.

CHAPTER TWO

TECHNICAL APPRAISAL OF THE TYPE 44 CHASSIS

Bugatti was at once ingenious and yet conservative. He clearly relished a technical problem, and plenty of sketches by his hand give testament to his ability to communicate his solutions. The extent to which these solutions were informed by physics or mathematics is less clear.

Bugatti settled on a standard for the chassis layout of his road cars quite early on. From the time of the chain drive 5-litre and Type 13, he specified conventional semi-elliptic front springs coupled with his patented reverse quarter-elliptic rear arrangement, so named because the rear springs face forward from the abutments on the chassis (Système Bugatti). This formula was to be sustained until the end of his life. The Type 44 embodies many other conservative characteristics and was an evolutionary link in Bugatti's haut-couture chain.

Power for the 44 is provided by an immensely tractable 69mm x 100mm, 3-litre straight-eight, which was new for the 44 and, in effect, a doubling of the four-cylinder Types 37/40 engine. This design brought forward many of the details of the 2-litre straight-eight that powered the Type 30 and its derivatives, while being more robust. A noteworthy feature of the Type 44 engine is the central camshaft drive, popular in some later 8-cylinder high-performance engines, but which did not appear among later Molsheim products. The clutch and separate gearbox drew directly from earlier models.

The engine is rigidly mounted and provides a stiff connection between the parallel sections of the chassis side rails. Additionally, cross connection of the frame is provided by further crossmembers amidships, supporting the gearbox forward of the rear axle between the damper mounts and the cross tube between the dumb irons. Thus far the description might evoke many a vehicle of the period, though the fact that all of these crossmembers are tubular instead of open U-section is less common, and the manner in which their attachment to the sidemembers is achieved is typical of Bugatti. The forged and brazed-on bosses are a clear indication that their contribution to the frame's torsional stiffness was not lost on Bugatti. The visible front spring hanger forging is particularly refined.

The real hallmark of Bugatti's chassis frames is the less conspicuous cross tube, often hidden by coachwork, between the two rear spring fixings. Although used by Lanchester, this feature is uncommon among designs of the day and makes a great contribution to rigidity, especially in torsion, while directly distributing suspension loads between the sidemembers. In fact, the conclusion is inescapable that Bugatti prized chassis frame torsional stiffness just as much as later generations of designers. Again, the loads are transmitted between this tube and the chassis sidemembers by well-proportioned forgings, brazed to the tube and provided with an ample ring of bolts. By positioning this tube at the rear of the chassis not only did he place it just where it would be most effective in distributing suspension loads, but also where it could be dead straight. His contemporaries most often relied on open-section crossmembers that have negligible torsional stiffness, positioned where they would interfere with the prop shaft or rear axle if they were straight.

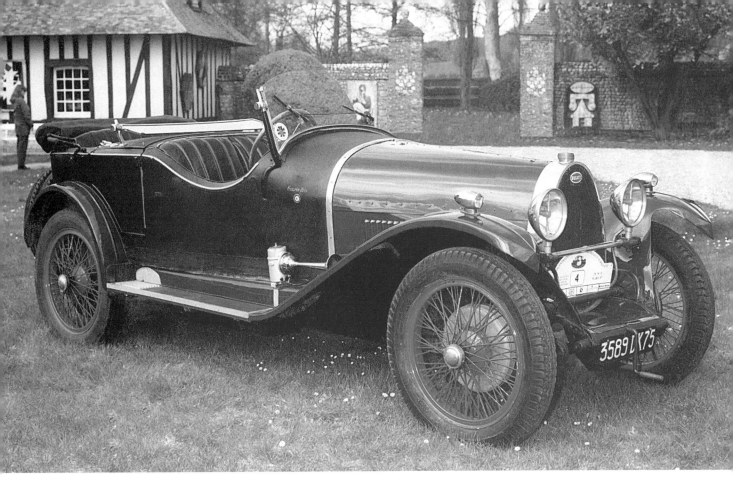

Type 30 chassis number 4314. Body by Kelsch, type Weymann. This car has had only three owners since 1923; the present owner purchased it in 1957.

Type 30 chassis numéro 4314. Carrosserie Kelsch, type Weymann. Cette voiture n'a eu que trois propriétaires depuis 1923. Le propriétaire actuel l'a achetée en 1957.

As a result, their contribution to chassis rigidity is naturally compromised.

Without doubt one of the greatest strengths of Molsheim's car maker was the ability to match or usually surpass the structural performance of its competitors while being more economical with material. The delight which is driving a Bugatti, the light precise steering and the sure-footed and progressive road holding, is the manifestation of this efficiency.

Perhaps the most quoted example of the lengths to which Bugatti was happy to go in pursuit of efficiency is the tubular front axle, almost straight, to avoid castor angle changes under braking. These axles were hollow in the case of the racing cars, the ultimate refinement. Again Bugatti exploits the efficiency of a tubular section, although at first sight it may not appear as entirely ideal for managing the bending loads set up by the wheels and springs. When we begin to consider the fore/aft loads due to potholes and braking, however, a round section seems more rational. Furthermore,

under braking there is a considerable torsional load, again best managed by a tubular section. Hollow sections were, of course, de rigeur for smaller components, such as track rods and cross shafts, among vintage designers, but those of a Bugatti typically have thinner walls and often larger diameters.

The steel of the front axle, its springs, and all the smaller steering components, as well as those of the braking system, was polished. Not only was this Bugatti elevating his engineered products to an art form, but also his pursuit of efficiency once again, as a polished surface renders the component measurably less susceptible to fatigue. This is the phenomenon whereby repeated loading propagates defects within the metallic structure, gradually reducing the component's ability to support its service load.

Akin to its siblings, the steering geometry of the 44 is discernibly Bugatti, due to its pronounced positive camber, but does not stray from convention otherwise. The chassis engineer of today might predict the positive camber to lead to

Chassis number 38397, now in the USA; coachbuilder unknown.
Type 38 numéro 38397, actuellement aux Etats-Unis. Carrossier inconnu.

Chassis number 44694, with, we believe, a replacement body, but with the correct 1929 style.
Type 44 numéro 44694. La carrosserie n'est sans doute pas d'origine, mais bien dans le style de 1929.

understeer. Modern cars, passenger or racing, are, however, designed to work on smooth tarmac, and to fit relatively wide tyres. Bugatti settled on his 'layout' at a surprisingly young age, when roads were unmettled and tyres were narrow, beaded-edged, and when a car's balance was not so much a matter of tyre contact. It seems remarkable, therefore, that

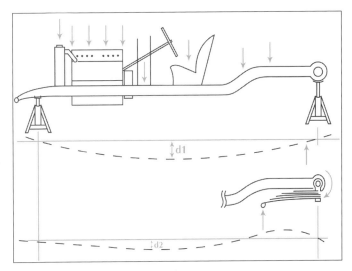

Force diagram.
Diagramme de flexion.

This page & opposite top: It has proved possible to achieve a high mileage with a Type 30 or 38, without reliability problems, providing the owner has a high degree of sensitivity for machinery, avoids the bad vibration periods, and is punctilious with oil changes and filter cleansing. Jean Feray has so far completed 100,000 kilometers in his Type 30, chassis number 4352, which he has owned for fifty years. Note the dynamo drive and cast aluminium bulkhead common to the Type 30 only.

Cette page et tableau de bord ci-contre: Il est possible d'atteindre un kilométrage important avec un Type 30 ou 38, sans problème majeur de fiabilité si le conducteur connait très bien la voiture, évite les périodes de vibration du moteur et change régulièrement l'huile et nettoie les filtres à huile. Jean Feray a fait plus de 100.000Km sur son Type 30 (chassis numéro 4352) qu'il possède depuis plus de 50 ans. Remarquer la courroie de commande de dynamo et la cloison pare-feu en alliage léger coulé.

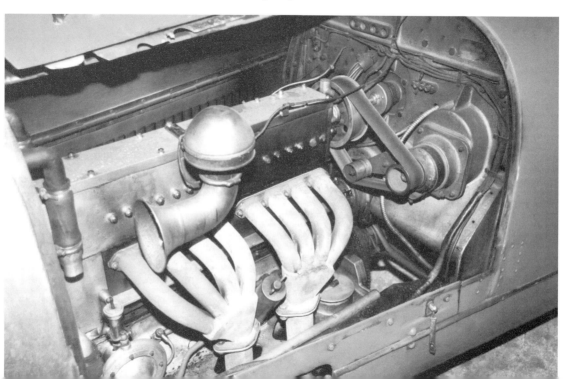

Below: Chassis number 38340 fitted with very neat and stylish faux cabriolet
by Lavocat et Marsaud with Fiacre elements.
Ci-dessous: Chassis numéro 38340 avec une carrosserie faux cabriolet d'un excellent dessin de Lavocat et Marsaud,
avec quelques éléments de Type Fiacre.

A factory publicity shot of a Bugatti-designed and built four-seater tourer, showing an American influence. Unusual hub-nuts and bonnet rear-edged line. The body is fully valenced, with step boards instead of running boards, folding rear deck and screen. This car could be a Type 38.

Photo destinée à une publicité; voiture de tourisme montrant une influence américaine. Ecrous de roue d'un Type inhabituel et capot spécial.

decades later the set up provides such a well-balanced car using tyres with markedly different characteristics. No doubt the expected understeer from the large positive camber acts as a foil for the oversteer that tends to dominate the behaviour of the front-engined, rear-wheel drive layout.

Conceptually, the rigid rear axle is conventional, but differs most noticeably in how the chassis is suspended from it. Bugatti's choice of the 'reverse' quarter elliptic spring, i.e. fixed to the rear extremity of the frame and running forward to its fulcrum on the axle, was unusual, and it is

interesting to speculate on his motive here. This layout has a significant impact on the bending moments in the chassis frame. In contrast to the semi-elliptic arrangement, which at rest passes purely vertical loads into the chassis at four points, Bugatti's system introduces a large turning moment to the chassis at the spring trunnion. This moment, as it happens, opposes and cancels that set up by the weight of the coachwork and payload. This allows the rear part of the chassis sidemembers to be lighter for a given deflection.

When we consider the influence of this system on ride and

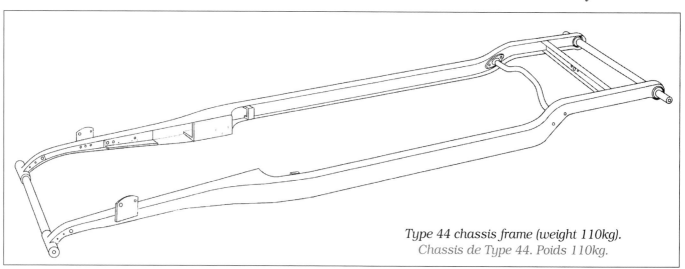

Type 44 chassis frame (weight 110kg).
Chassis de Type 44. Poids 110kg.

A Gangloff tourer; note the Bugatti style wings and unusual 'V' screen: clearly something is amiss with the bonnet scuttle line. Chassis number unknown.
Numéro de chassis inconnu. Aile de style Bugatti et pare-brise en 'V' inhabituel par Gangloff. Dessin moyen du capot.

A Type 30, chassis number 4725, recently fitted with a new touring body but correct in style for the early twenties.
Type 30, chassis numéro 4725; voiture récemment recarrossée dans le style des années 20.

A Type 38, chassis 38260, with well done replica roadster coachwork in the correct style.

Chassis numéro 38260 avec une carrosserie récente de roadster.

handling, we can uncover the main motive for its adoption. For good steering and safe control, excessive pitching and rolling of the body is to be avoided. By supporting the spring mass as far rearward as is possible, maximum control over pitching is achieved and the high position of the rear fixings gives good roll control. Bugatti learned his craft at a time which was not only the dawn of motoring but the twilight of the horse-drawn carriage, and he had a love of both horse and carriage. Centuries of experience had been gained by the carriage makers, not least in the matter of ride and suspension. Bugatti would have undoubtedly relished bringing this knowledge to bear in the new era.

By Hugh Price, MSC

Elizabeth Junek and friend in her first Bugatti Type 30. The radiator shape appears to be of Type 28 style. Chassis number 4001.

Elisabeth Junek et une amie dans sa première Bugatti de Type 30; le radiateur semble être d'un Type 28. Chassis numéro 4001.

An early Type 30 engine on the works test bench; this engine is fitted with twin Zenith carburettors.

Moteur de Type 30 de première série sur le banc d'essai de l'usine; avec deux carburateurs Zenith.

CRANKSHAFT DAMPERS

The Achilles heel of the straight-eight engine concerns crankshaft torsional vibration. This phenomenon can best be described as a winding and unwinding of the shaft which occurs at several progressive periods of engine speed.

All engines suffer from this condition to an extent, but the length of the crankshaft of the eight-in-line configuration exacerbates the problem.

The addition of a form of flexible mass to the shaft, suitably designed, will bring down the vibration to an acceptable level. One might liken this effect to that of placing one's finger on a violin string. A form of flywheel, which is allowed to slip within limits, is the most expedient way to success.

The Type 30 did not possess a damper and, as described elsewhere, was abominably rough. The Type 38 similarly did not possess a damper, but the heavy 'dyno-starter' attached to the crankshaft nose may have had a beneficial effect. The author does not possess experience of the type.

Several schemes were tried on the first batch of 3-litre Type 44 engines, but the production cars were all fitted with an unusual device, which was satisfactory when in good adjustment.

This damper consisted of a flange spigoted onto the nose of the crankshaft, which held six pegs onto which rubber bushes were placed. An outer flywheel was located on these bushes and, in turn, was held in place by a face plate with a friction disc interposed. The whole assembly was pressed against the rubber bushes by a large nut on the crankshaft. The amount of compression of the rubber bushes governs the success of the damper.

Loading figures were never issued by the factory as far as we know. No doubt much trial and error took place before the skilled engine fitters obtained the right 'feel', so to speak. The damper was to continue right until the end of the Type 49 production.

The Bugatti Trust holds a set of drawings for a conventional friction damper, all numbered in the Type 49 series but apparently never issued for production. It incorporated two flywheels, which clamped to a central disc with fibre friction plates in between and spring loaded. This was almost identical to the Rolls-Royce system. The following Type 57 was fitted with an enlarged version of the type. Again, no pressure or loading figures were ever issued.

By Barrie Price

Type 44 crankshaft damper exposed.

Amortisseur de vibrations situé à l'avant d'un vilebrequin de Type 44. La partie avant en métal a été décalée pour montrer les cylindres en caoutchouc.

The engine of chassis number 49466, a low mileage original car, showing the twin plug layout and original American Schebler carburettor.

Moteur du chassis 49466; la voiture a un kilométrage réduit. On peut voir l'allumage à deux bougies par cylindre et le carburateur Schebler d'origine américaine.

Type 49 showing the central drive for the camshaft. This car has a non-standard modern inlet scheme.
Moteur de Type 49 montrant l'arbre vertical de commande de l'arbre à cames. Ce moteur a une pipe d'admission d'un modèle spécial.

A rare chassis assembly shop photograph shows both Types 44 and 49 in the course of build, presumably at the point of changeover to the 3.3-litre car in late 1930/early 1931.

Une rare photo de l'atelier des chassis où sont montés des Types 44 et 49; la photo a dû être prise au moment du changement de modèle fin 1930 début 31 (entre les 3l et les 3,3l)

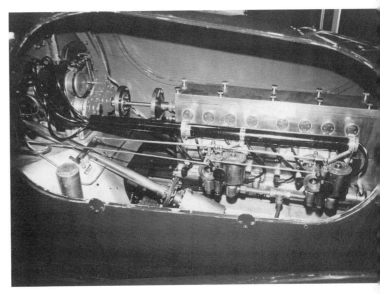

The Type 30 engine in the Strasbourg Grand Prix car of 1922. This is a recent picture of the car after restoration, chassis 4002. Note the twin Zenith carburettors and the cylindrical reservoir for the front hydraulic brake fluid at left.

Moteur de Type 30 utilisé au Grand Prix de Strasbourg de 1922. Chassis numéro 4002. Photographie récente après restauration. Remarquer les deux carburateurs Zenith et à gauche le réservoir cylindrique pour les freins avant hydrauliques.

Type 30 cockpit. Note the unusual brake pedal for hydraulic operation.

Type 30. Pédale spéciale pour les freins hydrauliques.

Jean Bugatti with his young brother Roland about to road test a Type 38 chassis; note dyna-motor not yet fitted. Tyres appear to be oversize with strange tread pattern.

Jean Bugatti et son jeune frère Roland avant un essai d'un chassis Type 38. Le dynastart (appareil combinant dynamo et démarreur) n'est pas encore monté. Pneus Type «ballon» avec des sculptures d'un dessin inhabituel.

An early Type 49 undergoing chassis testing. Houdaille dampers visible at the rear.

Type 49 de début de série aux essais. Les amortisseurs Houdaille sont visibles à l'arrière.

A later Type 49 on a delivery run, note the different, by one digit, tradeplate compared with the previous photograph. One imagines that the works must have had at least five or six sets of tradeplates when at the height of production.

Un autre Type 49 en livraison. L'usine avait un certain nombre de plaques provisoires, dont seul le dernier numéro différait.

The works fire engine constructed from a Type 44 chassis; it would appear to be grossly overladen at the rear. A chassis number was never issued because the vehicle was retained for works use, even travelling to Bordeaux with the works equipment in September 1939.

Voiture de pompiers de l'usine de Type 44. La voiture semble surchargée à l'arrière. On pense que le chassis n'a jamais reçu de numéro parce que la voiture ne quittait pas l'usine; elle fut pourtant transportée à Bordeaux en septembre 1939 avec une partie des machines de l'usine.

Type 49 wheel. Each cast aluminium wheel carried its own number.

Roue de Type 49; chaque roue en aluminium porte un numéro martelé.

Development of the 8-cylinder engine: Note the differing sump designs for cooling the oil. The orignal Type 30 dynamo was driven by a belt from the rear of the camshaft. The Type 38 was notable for the use of a combined dynamo and starter situated on the front of the crankshaft. Types 44 and 49 retained a dynamo driven from the crankshaft, but reverted to a traditional starter, which engaged with the flywheel. The camshaft on Types 44 and 49 was centrally-driven, thus minimising torsional effects on this component.

Evolution des moteurs 8-cylindres: Remarquer le dessin différent des carters pour le refroidissement de l'huile. Dynastart à l'avant du vilebrequin pour le Type 38, dynamo pour les Types 44 et 49 qui ont un amortisseur de vibrations du vilebrequin. Les 44 et 49 ont un arbre a cames dont l'arbre vertical de commande passe entre les deux blocs, pour éviter des efforts de torsion de l'arbre à cames.

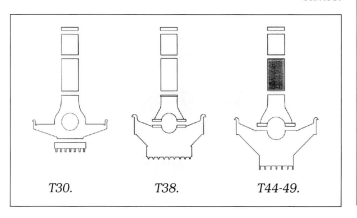

T30.   T38.   T44-49.

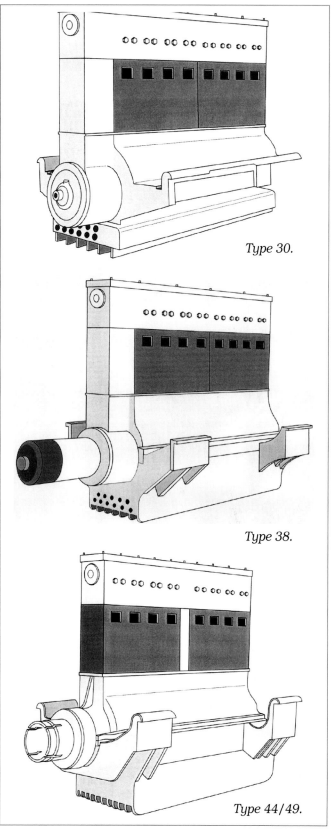

Type 30.

Type 38.

Type 44/49.

Rear view of Type 30 engine showing integral mounting of steering box on crankcase.
Arrière d'un moteur de Type 30; le boîtier de direction est boulonné sur le carter.

TYPE 30 ENGINE COMPONENTS

The crankshaft is installed through the front of the crankcase.

Crankshaft machined from solid billet and in two sections in order to fit the centre ball race.
Le Vilebrequin est en deux parties usinées dans la masse; elles sont réunies dans le roulement à billes central.

The sump complete with cooling tubes.
Le carter est boulonné après le montage des bielles.

CHAPTER THREE

SOME THOUGHTS ON BUGATTI DESIGN POLICY

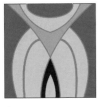

The arrival of the Type 35 racing car in 1924 heralded the pinnacle of detail refinement that could be seen in all subsequent designs as well as the main subject of this work. Bugatti's policy was to simplify and complete a design with as few parts as possible.

We can illustrate one detail, unique in the experience of the author. This concerns the levers or arms relating to track rod and drag links. Bugatti manufactured these parts as one piece items, the ball ends being integral with the arms. These items were forged flat and machined, including the refined, if expensive, 'flat taper' (least stress narrow width, maximum stress wide width). This latter feature necessitated another expensive operation in boring out the corresponding apertures of the mating components. Following the machining operations the ball neck was bent, subjected to heat treatment and protective plating. The ball and neck, together with the threaded stud at the opposite end, appear to have been masked out to prevent plating in the interests of avoiding any possible hydrogen embrittlement.

This elegant scheme necessitates changing the entire arm when the ball becomes worn, instead of the replacement of a detachable ball pin, which is the case with every other maker. The answer Bugatti would undoubtedly give if questioned by the service department as to the wisdom of the one piece design, would be to say; "If an owner can afford one of my cars, he can well afford to buy a new arm when the time arrives!" In practice, the arm would not become in need of replacement until a high mileage had been covered, and the great majority of the cars would by then be in the hands of a third or fourth owner.

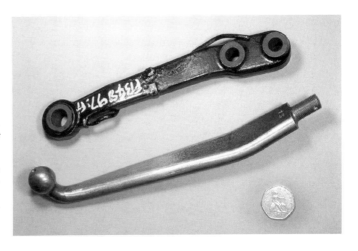

Below: Typical Bugatti track rod arm. Above: Bentley/ Rolls-Royce track rod arm (1947-1955). Superior 'H' section but inelegant in appearance; note the inferior method of attachment by two bolts in shear.

En dessous: Pièce de Bugatti. En haut: Même pièce pour Rolls-Royce ou Bentley (1947-1955): section en H correcte, mais dessin peu élégant; boulons travaillant en cisaillement.

CHAPTER FOUR

BUGATTI TYPE 33 – A CAR OR LIGHT LORRY?

Conceived during the early 1920s, the Type 33 is one of Ettore's little known but intriguing designs. Apart from the engine which was the 2-litre, 8-cylinder Type 30, nearly all the parts were newly designed specifically for the Type 33.

It was the first Molsheim product to be fitted with the fully compensated cable-operated 4-wheel brakes which were such an important feature of the later cars.

The Type 33 chassis frame was the first to have curved side rails to allow more useful space within the frame. The same side rails were later called up for the Type 43.

The steering box was of a new design which was subsequently used for the touring cars and the Type 43, and which was only slightly modified for the Grand Prix cars.

Bugatti conceived the Type 33 as a development of the Type 30 but with more of the chassis length available for passenger accommodation or light lorry payload behind the front seats. To achieve this, he moved the driving position forwards. The flywheel and clutch were contained in a separate aluminium casing under the front seats in order to create more room for the driver's feet and pedals immediately behind the engine. At the same time, a front lowered footwell provided a more upright driving position so that the front seats could be even further forwards. Bugatti patented these two ideas on 27th September 1923 – see the accompanying illustrations from French patent number 571219.

For the Type 33, Bugatti used a gearbox in unit with the back axle, similar to his Type 32. Most of what we know of the details of the Type 33 design comes from the original

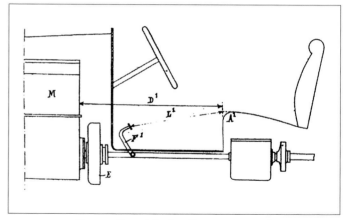

Conventional footwell arrangement.
Position habituelle dés pédales et du siège.

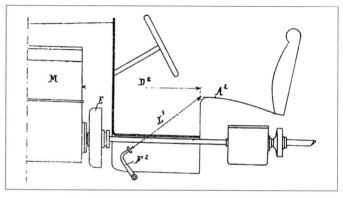

Front footwell with a more forward driving position.
Pédales et siège du conducteur avancés.

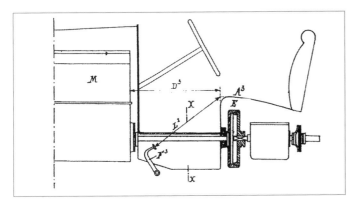

The same but with the clutch and flywheel moved back, under the seats, further reducing the necessary distance between the back of the engine and the front of the seat. *L'embrayage et le volant-moteur sont reculés sous le siège pour réduire l'écartement nécesssaire entre l'arrière du moteur et l'avant du siège.*

as distinct from a normal Type 30 by the cast aluminium front footwell and the absence of side mounted handbrake and gear levers.

CONCLUSION

As a development of the 30, the Type 33 was a 2-litre, 8-cylinder road car or light lorry with maximum payload space for the given chassis length. The radiator, chassis frame, steering and braking systems were new designs which were subsequently used for several of the touring cars, variously, the Types 38, 38A, 40, 43 and 44.

By Richard Day

The inherent roughness of the Type 30 engine would be exacerbated with the remote flywheel mass, while the torsional loads on the connecting shaft would be very high.

By Barrie Price

This sketch has been produced with reference to the individual component drawings. It shows a cast aluminium bulkhead positioned immediately aft of the engine crankcase. There is a deep, cast aluminium front footwell complete with all the footbrake pedal shafts and all the new brake compensating mechanism and the handbrake with its cross-shaft levers. This whole sub-assembly could be offered up and bolted to the lower flange of the chassis frame side rails. The flywheel and clutch were within a separate casing which also bridged across the chassis frame and incorporated useful storage bins under the front seats. The carden shaft required a polished nickel plated steel tube to protect the driver's and front passenger's legs within the footwell. (Courtesy Richard Day)

Bugatti drawings and parts lists. Like the Type 28, the gearlever was mounted centrally, operating the rear mounted gearbox via straight rods.

The type 33 factory camionette can be positively identified

At least one Type 33 was actually built as a factory camionette which was photographed at the 1924 French Grand Prix at Lyon – the famous debut of the Type 35 racing cars.
Un Type 33 au moins a été construit. Il a été utilisé comme camionnette et photographié au Grand Prix de Lyon de 1924, première course du célèbre Type 35.

CHAPTER FIVE

NEW CAR PRICES

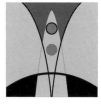

BUGATTI CHASSIS PRICES IN FRANCE

1926	Type 30	2000cc	42,100F	
1928	Type 38	2000cc	53,200F	
1929	Type 38A	blown	75,000F	
1930	Type 44	3000cc	60,000F	
1930	Type 49	3300cc	63,000F	Short chassis
1931	Type 49	3300cc	63,500F	Long chassis
	Type 49		Supplement for alloy wheels: 3000F	

There were no other 8-cylinder cars of this capacity on the French market at this period.

SOME PRICES FOR COMPLETE 6-CYLINDER FRENCH CARS

1928	Talbot DUS	2600cc	76,400F
1929	Hotchkiss AM 80	3000cc	56,600F
1929	Peugeot 6 cyl		39,800F
1930	Delahaye	3230cc	43,300F
1932	Citroen C6	2650cc	33,500F
1934	Renault Vivasix	3000cc	32,500F

The only foreign makes which had agencies in France at this time and sold cars comparable with Bugatti were (chassis and coachwork):

1927	Alfa Romeo RL 22/90	3000cc	75,000F
1929	Rolls Royce 20HP	3127cc	100,000F
1934	Bentley 3½ litre	3559cc	100,000F

All those French and foreign cars were 6-cylinders; Renault and Citroën had modest side-valve engines and were the top models of mass-produced lines, which explains their low prices. From this list it's easy to understand that Bugattis were more expensive than cars of other makes which, with their formal black coachwork, were the normal choice of the French bourgeoisie.

Year	Type	Chassis	4-Seater Tourer	Sportsman 'S' Coupé	Saloon
1930	Type 44	£575.00	£800.00	£860.00	£915.00
1931	Type 49	£625.00	£850.00	£910.00	£965.00
1932	Type 49	£700.00	£850.00	£910.00	£965.00

The price of standard coachwork could vary from 20 per cent (2-seater Roadster) to 50 per cent of the total price.

EQUIVALENT BRITISH CARS 1929-30

No comparable 8-cylinder cars were marketed except for a rarity in the form of the Arrol-Aster 24/80 single sleeve valve car.

Make and model	Capacity	Chassis	Saloon
Sunbeam 20.9	2.9 litre	£595.00	£875.00
Sunbeam 3 litre	3 litre	£995.00	£1075.00
Alvis Silver Eagle	2.2 litre	£500.00	£695.00
MG 18/80	2.5 litre	£455.00	£565.00
Talbot 75	2.3 litre	£425.00	£595.00

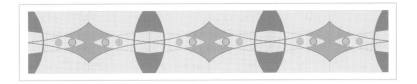

CHAPTER SIX

THE RESTORATION OF A TYPE 49

After 45 years with a Type 40, and a good 30,000km with it, it seemed normal to offer more comfort to one's wife and give more power to the driver.

An open car with a good protection against rain and room for passengers and luggage was researched. An eight-cylinder like a 44 or 49 was an obvious choice. I finally found a 49 which, with other cars, stayed in a heated garage; it had not been used for more than 20 years.

The car was unpainted but had had primer on all the steel parts, which had not rusted. Above all the wood frame was absolutely perfect, and its original paint was as new. As the car had not been driven for so many years, it was decided to dismantle it to the last nut and bolt.

The wiring had to be completely changed, similarly with upholstery and hood; the old items were used as models.

The mechanic and coachbuilder being sixty kilometres apart, it was decided to leave the engine and gearbox to the mechanic and to transport the frame and the body to the coachbuilder. My work was to find the missing parts and to transport them to the two workshops; twenty different suppliers were used and, in twenty months 3500 kilometres were travelled. Sketches were made for all parts; plating added up to 120 parts; every supplier had a file with the promised delivery dates, and all phone calls were noted.

The car was bought in December 1997 and I had set myself a target. To be ready for the June 1999 Bugatti International Rallye, which was organised by the French Bugatti club, a diary was kept:

December 1997: Car inspected by mechanic and coachbuilder.

January 1998: Engine and gearbox dismantled, seats and hood seen by upholsterer; instruments brought to a specialist; first batch to be plated to the supplier; boot modification sketched.

February 1998: Parts (locks, rear lights) bought at Retromobile; engine dismantled; crankshaft balanced by specialist; coachwork separated from chassis; paint from both removed; panel beating for the boot inspected.

March 1998: Instruments ready; second batch to be plated to supplier; parts for engine ordered; pistons, valves and springs, camshaft. Chassis back to mechanic; front axle dismantled and checked (magnaflux).

April 1998: Front axle and steering wheel to plating; coachwork finished; front axle and front dampers mounted.

May 1998: Chassis painted; crankcase, gearbox and rear axle bolted on chassis. Work on water and oil pumps; starter and dynamo brought to specialist; plated parts delivered to coachmaker; choice of colours made; windscreen and all glasses ordered.

June 1998: Chassis back to coachmaker; painting finished, rear wings and glass mounted.

July 1998: Car back to mechanic; work on engine and brakes; dashboard fitted; new wiring and fuses fitted.

August 1998: Holiday!

September 1998: Radiator, steering and rear dampers mounted. First rolling test.

October 1998: Car back to coachmaker; front wings, bumpers, spare wheel hub and lights mounted; steel part of steering wheel and chestnut cabinet parts to specialist. Stainless exhaust and petrol tank ordered.

November 1998: Car back to mechanic; new carburettor, instruments, switches and fuses tested.

December 1998: Wheels polished, rear tyres changed; new camshaft fitted.

January 1999: Horn push, warning switch and swivelling light fitted. Car registered.

February 1999: Car sent by lorry to Holland to fit overdrive.

March 1999: Car back to Paris.

April 1999: Car with upholsterer for hood, seats, carpets and fitting of cabinet parts.

June 1999: 12 June trip of 150km: 13 June Paris-Poitiers 330km: Start of the rally!

By Jean-Louis Arbey

Type 49, chassis number 49248. Drophead coupé by Chiattone of Lugano, prior to restoration in 1998.
Type 49 numéro 49248. Coupé décapotable par Chiattone de Lugano, en 1998 avant sa restauration.

First test.
Premier essai.

Jean-Louis and Martine Arbey in the same car after restoration.
Jean-Louis et Martine Arbey dans la même 49, restauration terminée.

CHAPTER SEVEN

ORDERING A BUGATTI IN THE THIRTIES

 In the nineteen-thirties there were a number of options open to the potential Bugatti purchaser. They could place their order directly with Molsheim, for example, or through one of the many Bugatti agents found throughout Europe. One could even place an order in one of the Salons de l'Automobile where the marque was being displayed.

Customers had the choice of a catalogue car, with a body made either by the works or by a coachbuilder, such as Gangloff of Colmar or Jarvis in England, though the colour, including that of the interior leather, and many details could be suited to an owner's tastes, as could the tyres and lights (Marchal, Scintilla, Bosch or Grebel, for example). In fact, there was a seemingly endless list of accessories, and some types, such as the 30 or 49, could be bought with a short or long chassis. The 49, for example, could be ordered with either Rudge wire or (rather beautiful) alloy wheels.

If a customer, or his wife, wanted something special, then he had to order a chassis. These were almost always delivered by road, driven by intrepid mechanics heavily clad in leather ex-French Air Force jackets and trousers (many of the drivers had done their two years' Service in one of the many airfields located along the German frontier). The car left the works complete from bonnet to bulkhead, with lights, but without a windscreen!

French and foreign coachbuilders were aplenty at this time, and as Bugatti was exporting much of what he produced, chassis could go to Britain, Germany, Switzerland, Belgium, Italy, Czechoslovakia, the USA and Argentina.

With the coachbuilder, draughtsmen were able to submit different sketches which could be amended to suit the buyer's taste. The customer could ask for a classical type of coachwork (wooden frame and metal) or the Weymann patent (light wooden frame and pvc) or all metal (de Vizcaya patent).

Coachbuilders in big towns were often in the same district or in a nearby suburb. The work was labour intensive, workers often doing between 45 and 50 hours per week, with apprentices sometimes only 14 years old.

All the shops were working with wood and metal. They also had forges and were able to manufacture body hardware, although outside suppliers offered door locks, handles and so forth. Plating was usually done by specialists. Wooden frames were usually in ash; though some coachbuilders, like Chapron and Figoni in Paris used beech, which was cheaper but less durable.

Workers were able to go from blueprints to a finished car in a very short time, sometimes two months after the chassis delivery. Customers who had chosen a coachbuilder near their home could drop in from time to time to see the progress of the work and frequently change the specification.

The coachbuilder had to agree to what the customer wanted, and, as a result, some cars had ugly or rather curious aerodynamic lines. Some orders were very strange. Colonel Sorel, for example, the main Bugatti importer, had a limousine built by Harrington which was high enough to allow him to drive wearing a bowler hat!

Painting the cars was a lengthy process, particularly during the paint and varnish era, though cellulose began to take over in the early thirties. Many cars were black, but open cars often had lighter colours.

For a Concours d'Elegance, it was common for some ladies to first chose the shades of their dresses, and ask the coachmaker to match the colour to the car.

Coachbuilders had catalogues for windscreen frames, bumpers, wheel discs, door and window handles, for limousine trunks and folding seat mechanisms, as well as interior pulls, which the French called 'dowager straps'.

Smokers or ladies companion 'nécessaire' and small flower vases were also available, often in silver. As the bodies were built on wooden frames, panelled by hand or covered in fabric, which enjoyed a vogue in the late '20s, a coachbuilder rarely made two identical bodies.

We know of some cars which had their original coachwork discarded; and chassis could even be shortened, like a Type 49 which received a very light body by Bertelli in England.

Large firms like Labourdette in Paris could make their own upholstery and marquetry, but this work for dashboard, doors and division of chauffeur-driven cars was often the work of the best cabinet-makers.

Rare woods were used, as were ivory and tortoiseshell. The latter was specified by Mr Esders, for his wife's

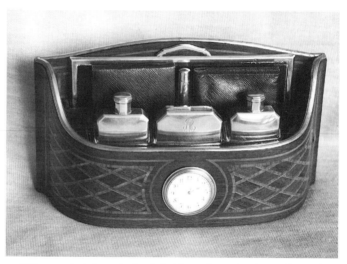

'Nécessaire' for a lady, inlaid work and silver gilt, with mirror, powder box and perfume bottles.
Nécessaire, marquetterie et vermeil, avec miroir, poudrier et flacons de parfum.

Rolls-Royce Phantom II. This car was sold in 2004 at an auction in France.

By Jean-Louis Arbey

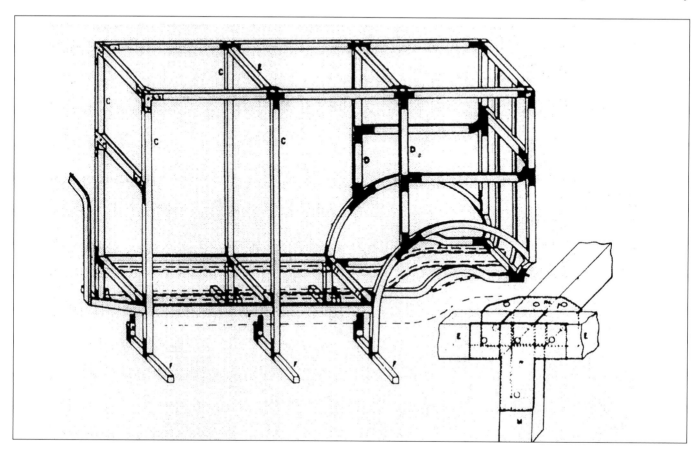

38

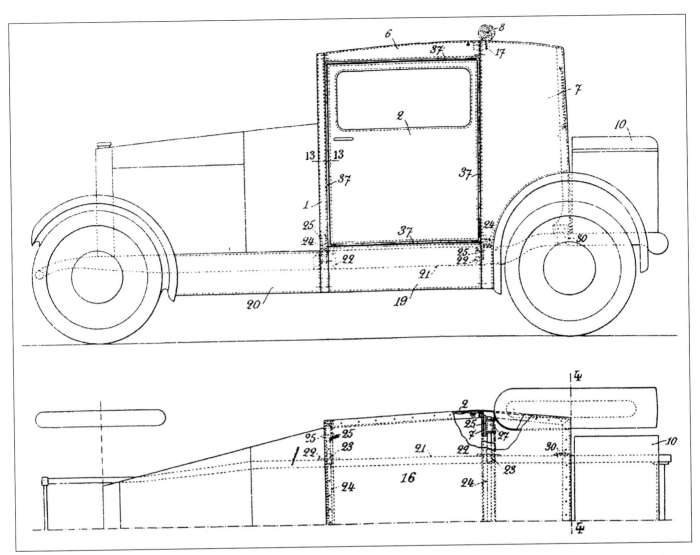

Patent Vizcaya, used by Million-Guiet, Paris. This technique involved body manufacture by way of metal panels bolted together and without a separate frame, apart from simple channel sections. The body shapes were restricted to simple forms to avoid expensive press work. See photo page 41.

Système de carrosserie breveté par Vizcaya: tout l'ensemble est en métal (acier ou aluminium). Des panneaux de formes simples sont boulonnés entre eux: des pièces de montage sont prévus pour diminuer le bruit. Le profil de la carrosserie est rectangulaire pour éviter de coûteux emboutissages. Voir photo page 41.

Opposite: Patent diagram of Weymann body frame. Wood members are separated by metal plates to eradicate squeaks and allow some flexibility, hence the necessity of fabric (PVC) or leather on high quality bodies.

Dessin concernant le brevet du système de carrosserie Weymann: un cadre léger en sapin renforcé par des ferrures est ensuite recouvert à l'extérieur de simili-cuir et à l'intérieur par un bourrage de feutre, de coton et de crin, puis tapissé. Toutes les formes n'étaient pas possibles avec ce système, mais les carrosseries étaient légères et silencieuses.

CHAPTER EIGHT

CONCOURS D'ELÉGANCE

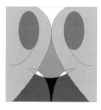

Between the First and Second World Wars, the Concours d'Elégance were part of high society life. Seaside resorts, spa towns, and many municipalities organized these events, which inhabitants and tourists

A magnificent Type 44 Sedança De Ville by a Parisian builder, we think Kellner or Binder, depicted at Longchamp.
Magnifique coupé 44 avec chauffeur d'un carrossier parisien, Kellner ou Binder, photographié à Longchamp, lors d'un Concours d'élégance.

An early Type 44 built by Million-Guiet under Vizcaya patents, photographed at a Concours d'Elegance in June 1928; note the expensive interior garnish rail work.

Type 44 carrossé par Million-Guiet sous licence Vizcaya et photographié à un Concours d'élégance en juin 1928. Remarquer l'excellente et coûteuse qualité de l'intérieur.

greatly enjoyed. Entrants could be the actualy owners of the cars, or even manufacturers and coachbuilders. Bugatti, for instance, entered the Royale on two occasions, and won a Grand Prix with one in Paris at Longchamp in 1929.

Most of the cars participating were of high quality; Rolls-Royce, Hispano, Delage, and forgotten makes such as Minerva, Horch or Packard, though cheaper cars also competed.

The Concours were not just for cars; they were also for the ladies (owners or passengers). All of them wore full-length gowns and wide-brimmed hats; and a styled attendant ceremoniously opened the door of their chauffeur-driven limousines.

The entrant could, of course, drive herself, and be with her children or her pet dogs, or both.

Many cups were given for different categories of car, and, normally, everyone was pleased with the results. Lengthy reports with plenty of pictures appeared in newspapers and magazines.

The Grand Prix was always the most coveted award, and some owners even ordered a car only to win it.

In one very important Concours, two ladies and their cars were possible winners. As everything was perfect, the president of the jury, a well known humorist, asked to see the engines; one was dirty, the other glowing. As he gave the prize to the latter car, the lady who had lost complained bitterly, saying that the rules did not state that the motor should be clean. The president replied; "Dear Madam, I neither wrote that your feet had to be washed ..."

The formula for winning a Grand Prix was: "une jolie voiture, une jolie femme, une jolie robe, et un joli chien!" (a pretty car, a pretty woman, a pretty dress, and a pretty dog!)

By Jean-Louis Arbey

Chassis number 44930, re-bodied in the mid-thirties and depicted in a Concours d'Elegance at La Baule in 1938. Note the judges on the left, and the capped chauffeur behind.

Chassis numéro 44930 recarrossé vers 1935 et photographié au Concours d'élégance de La Baule en 1938. Remarquer le jury à gauche et un chauffeur de maître avec sa casquette à l'arrière-plan.

CHAPTER NINE

EIGHT-CYLINDER TOURING CARS IN COMPETITION

The Types 30 and 38 touring cars did not figure strongly in competitive events, although the Junek husband and wife team did well in Czechoslovakia with one of the Strasbourg Type 30 Grand Prix cars fitted with a smart two-seater sports body, the first of several Bugattis with which this pair, particularly Elizabeth, achieved fame.

In 1922, Bugatti began to sell his first 8-cylinder production cars. The engine was able to attain very high revs (up to 5000) but was subject to bearing failure. The racing formula at that date was for engines up to 2-litres in size.

Bugatti produced a 2-seater racing version. The engine was fitted with two carburettors, twin magnetos and two plugs per cylinder, while the coachwork was designed by an Italian, Eduardo Moglia. Bugatti took second, third and fourth places at the Grand Prix de l'Automobile Club à Strasbourg on 10th July 1922. The winner, a Fiat with an advanced twin overhead camshaft, averaged 127kph (79.2mph) for the 800km race. Vizcaya was second at 111kmh (69.2mph) with Marco third at 102.6kph (63.8mph). Col Giles, President of the Bugatti Owners Club, ran a Type 38 in the popular London-Lands End Trials in 1932 and 1933, gaining a premier award in the latter year with a car then six or seven years old. He then transferred his affections to Type 49s fitted with English bodies, which were regularly campaigned. A Type 38 was known to compete at local events in Hanoi, then the capital of French Indo-China.

The Type 44 met with considerable success in long distance rallies, particularly Liège-Rome-Liège. The entrants in these events were most often Bugatti agents; Reinartz in Liège, Zigrand in Luxembourg, Lamberjack of Paris and Friderich of Nice. Orban won this event in 1932. There were twenty-four starters but only ten finished the long trip in this year. In later years, Trasenster and Breyre ran a lightweight and tuned Type 44 in these events between 1935 and 1939, actually winning the 1939 run outright, a formidable performance for a car then ten years old. We understand that the engine was highly tuned, running on high compression pistons, revised inlet manifolding and carburation, together with a high ratio rear axle.

Type 44 cars appeared in the prestigious Alpine Trials of the early 1930s. Several private owners took part in these events where they had to compete with many works sponsored teams. Sauerwein (Germany) and Schmid (Switzerland) the latter with a Type 49, took part in 1933 while Brio and Pucher and the brothers Descollas took part in 1934. None of these entrants, however, figured in the results, although a Type 43 supercharged sports car recorded the fastest acceleration and hill climb times in the 1933 event.

The Type 44 appeared in the Le Mans 24 Hour Race in 1934 and 1937, again the cars were well into old age; the 1934 entrants Desvignes and Mahé finished in ninth position averaging 67 miles per hour. The same pair won a ten hour Sports Car Race at Spa averaging 72½ miles per hour. Unfortunately, Kippeurth, the 1937 Le Mans entrant, suffered a fatal accident early in the race. Zigrand ran a highly modified Type 44 at Spa in 1929, and is said to have been timed at 183 kilometres per hour (113mph) which is

The first event for the 8-cylinder car in competition. The French Grand Prix, Strasbourg, 1922.
Première course d'une Bugatti 8-cylindres. Grand Prix de Strasbourg en 1922.

Two Type 32 racing cars undergoing assembly for the French Grand Prix held at Tours in 1923. Note the unusual radiator and chassis.
Deux voitures de course Type 32 préparées pour le Grand Prix de Tours (juillet 1923). Remarquer le radiateur et le chassis.

The Type 32 'Tank' after gaining third place in the Grand Prix of Automobile Club France.
Type 32 'Tank' arrivé troisième au Grand Prix de l'Automobile Club de France à Tours.

San Sebastian Touring Grand Prix 1924. Ferdinand de Vizcaya punctured his fuel tank early in the race, so his mechanic had to hold a petrol can up high to obtain a gravity feed for the rest of the race. Brother Pierre de Vizcaya is sitting on the pit counter. We consider this to be an early car still with hydraulic brakes. Type 30.

Grand Prix de Saint-Sébastien en 1924. Ferdinand de Vizcaya eut son réservoir percé dès le début de la course et son mécanicien dut tenir un bidon de pétrole assez haut pour alimenter le moteur pendant tout le reste de la course. Son frère Pierre est sur le stand. Voiture de début de série avec freins hydrauliques à l'avant. Type 30.

extraordinary. Several hill climb successes were achieved by the Type 44 in France and Switzerland.

The most impressive performance of a Type 44 concerns a full 4-door Saloon (Van Vooren), which underwent an endurance run at Montlhéry in April 1929 covering 3009 kilometres (1525 miles) and averaged 80.5 miles per hour including a fifteen minute pit stop. This run was a Bugatti publicity event using works drivers Divo, Marco and Dutilleux under the supervision of Jean Bugatti and Meo Costantini. The mechanical condition of all the components was inspected

after the run by representatives of the Automobile Club de France and were found to be in 'perfect condition'. This car was then subjected to further running and was found to ascend Mount Valérien "easily in top gear with four passengers aboard". A further stunt concerned Zigrand who drove between Luxembourg and Paris three times during a day in 1931 (2130 kilometres).

British garage proprietor, Arthur Baron, substantially modified a Type 44 in 1933, shortening the chassis and uprating the engine by way of fitting four Solex carburettors,

A Type 38 driven by Sandonino at the opening event at the first race of the Modena Circuit, Italy, in June 1927.
Type 38 conduit par Sandonino lors de la première course sur le circuit de Modène en juin 1927.

This picture shows the car at scrutineering, where wing wheel clearance seems to be undergoing a check; note the rough slave body fitted.
La voiture de Sandonino au contrôle technique pour la mesure de la distance entre la roue et l'aile. Construction de carrosserie très légère en arrière du capot.

A Type 44 driven by Philippe Rothschild in the 1929 Grand Prix de l'Automobile Club France, held at Le Mans. The race was run under a fuel consumption formula and this car finished third.

Type 44 conduit par Philippe Rothschild en 1929 au Grand Prix de l'Automobile Club au Mans. Le règlement de la course avait prévu une formule à la consommation; la voiture termina troisième.

lightening the flywheel, and fitting a single-seater body together with a gearbox from a grand prix car. His efforts resulted in winning the Bugatti Owners' Club Victor Ludorum Trophy. In post-war years A S (Bert) Raven appeared with a highly developed Type 44 engine, again with four carburettors, which he inserted in a Type 37 chassis. Raven lived near Arthur Baron and no doubt received his help and guidance.

The post-war years were to witness the painful sight of a Type 44 (44596) converted for use in stock car racing actually winning an award on at least one occasion. The most recent example of a special Type 44 used in competition is that of Bruce Stops who campaigns this car in current (2006) Vintage Sports Car Club events with great success.

By Barrie Price & Jean-Louis Arbey

The number of entries and victories of the Type 44 in races or rallies is impressive:

1929 A saloon body (Weymann) by Van Vooren covered 3009km in 24 hours at Montlhéry; the drivers were Divo, Marco, Dutilleux. The average speed was 125.39kph with 15 minutes only in the pits, under the supervision of Costantini, who was responsible for the racing drivers, and Jean Bugatti.
Grand Prix of the A C F at Le Mans, on a consumption formula.
Spa 24 hour race. The drivers were Barthélémy and Porta; 2108km; 9th overall.

1930 Monte Carlo Rally: Dony came 75th.
Paris-Deauville Rally won by the Marquis d'Aulan with the Type 44, chassis number 1052.
Spa 24 hour Race. The drivers were Evrard and Trasenster; 10th with 2045km.
Grand Prix d'Oran; Type 44s come 2nd and 3rd.

1931 Zigrand, with his mechanic Bouquet, drove three times in one day on open roads from Luxembourg to Paris, covering a distance of 2130km. He took his engine up to 6000rpm.

1932 Paris-Saint Raphaël with Mlle Friderich.
Klausen hillclimb in Switzerland with Scheibler.
Liège-Rome-Liège. Orban was 1st; ten finished out of twenty-four to start.

1933 Monte Carlo Rally: Type 44, chassis number 1313 retired, after having towed another car in the Pyrénées.

1934 Le Mans 24 hour race. The drivers were Desvignes and Mahé who came 9th. They covered 2584km (1605 miles) at an average speed of 107kph.
Spa 10 hour race. The drivers Desvignes and Mahé came 1st at an average speed of 116kph.

1935 Liège-Rome-Liège. Trasenster came 1st. Eight finished out of thirty-five at the start.

1936 Spa 24 hour race. Trasenster retires after four hours.
Grand Prix de Comminges. Kippeurth came 7th.

1935-36 Type 44 Chassis number 266 was fitted with Type 49 cylinder blocks and shortened chassis to win the Victor Ludorum of the Bugatti Owners' Club. (Best aggregate performances).

1937 Kippeurth is killed at Le Mans in a Type 44, chassis number 441235.

1937-38 Hill climbs of Majola and race at Bremgarten, Switzerland. Driven by Scheibler.

1938 Liège-Rome-Liège. Trasenster 1st. The road near Nancy had been covered with nails; eighteen finished out of fifty-six starters.

1939 Liège-Rome-Liège. Trasenster 1st. Twenty-one finished out of fifty-four starters.

Trasenster/Breyre in the Liège-Rome-Liège of 1935; the Type 44 won the event, an impressive performance for a seven year old car.

Trasenster/Breyre au Liège-Rome-Liège de 1935. Cette 44 gagna la course, un succès remarquable pour une voiture vieille de sept ans.

The start, Chinetti (Alfa Romeo) about to overtake Mahé, followed by Brunet/Zehender in a Type 55. Both Bugattis retired.

Au début de la course, Chinetti sur Alfa Romeo, suivi par la 55 de Brunet/Zehender, double Mahé. Ces deux Bugatti abandonnèrent.

Another Type 44 engaged in the Liège-Rome-Liège in 1932, driven by Orban and Havelange; note the rudimentary lightweight body fitted.

Autre Type 44 au Liège-Rome-Liège, avec une carrosserie très légère.

Le Mans 24-hour race 1934. Mahé/Desvignes with a Type 44. Photographed at the pits before the start. Note the lightweight wings and compulsory bonnet straps.

Course des 24 Heures du Mans de 1934. Mahé/Desvignes avec un Type 44 photographié devant les stands avant la course. Remarquer les garde-boue de petites dimensions et les courroies de capot obligatoires au Mans.

Another Type 44 competing in the 1938 Liège-Rome-Liège event resulting in another victory. The car is pictured in Rome.

Type 44 au Liège-Rome-Liège de 1938 où la voiture remporta une nouvelle victoire. Voiture photographiée à Rome.

King Leopold III congratulating the victors.
Le roi Léopold III félicite les vainqueurs.

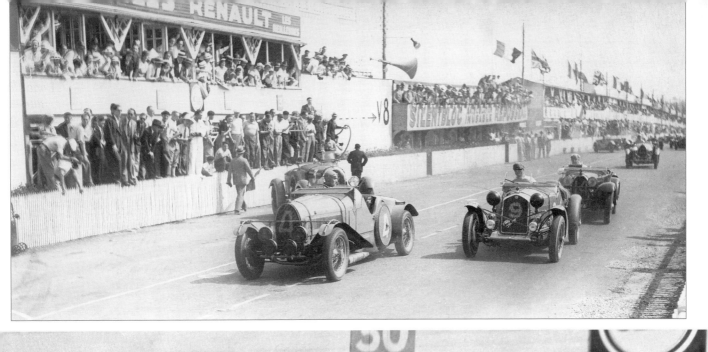

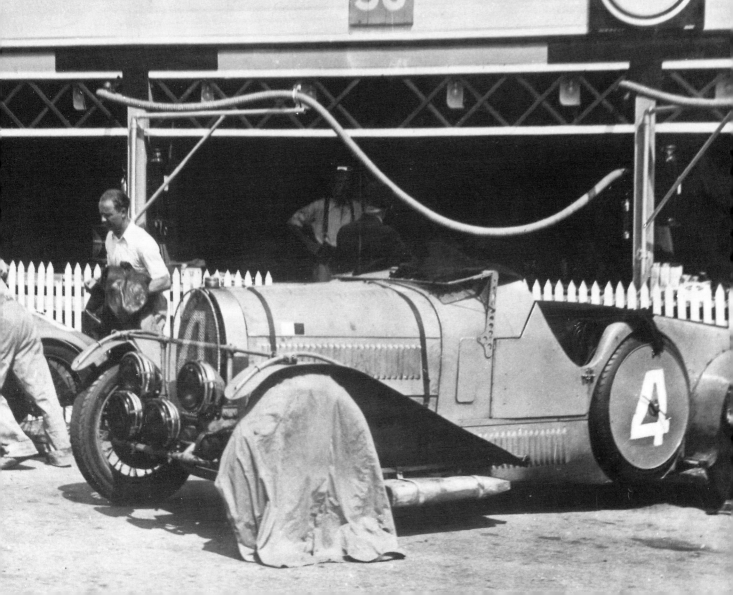

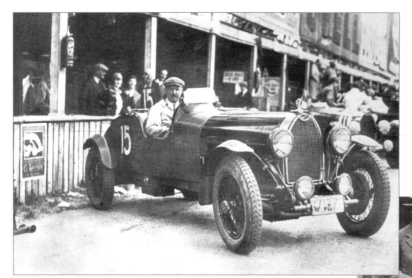

A Type 44 in a pre-war competition at Francorchamps, Belgium, 1929.
Type 44 en course avant guerre. Francorchamps. 1929.

Another Type 44 racing at Francorchamps, 1930.
Un autre Type 44 à Francorchamps. 1930.

Kippeurth in a Type 44 competing in a sports car event at Spa, Belgium in 1937; he was killed later that year at Le Mans.
Kippeurth sur Type 44 dans une course de voitures de sport en 1937, à Spa. Il se tua au Mans la même année.

Scheibler in a Type 44 competing at a hill climb event at La Maloja, Switzerland in 1938. The car was then ten years old.
Scheibler sur Type 44 dans une course de côte à Maloja (Suisse) en 1938. La voiture avait alors dix ans.

This page: An all-comers race at Montlhéry. The photograph on the right shows André Bith in a modernised Type 44, chassis number 44451.
Course à Montlhéry ouverte à tous. Le pilote André Bith sur Type 44 (chassis numéro 44451) modernisé.

54

Chassis number 44761. A Type 44 converted into a racing car, photographed outside the Jack Lemon-Burton house in north London, 1938. Chassis numéro 44761. Type 44 transformé en voiture de course photographié devant la maison de Jack Lemon-Burton au Nord de Londres en 1938.

We believe this is the same car, modified and used with great success for many years by A S Raven, at Prescott in May 1960. Note the four SU carburettors and the telescopic dampers.

Nous pensons que c'est la même voiture, après modifications, qui fut utilisée avec un grand succès par A S Raven pendant plusieurs années. Photo prise à Prescott en mai 1960. Remarquer les quatre carburateurs SU et les amortisseurs telescopiques.

A Weymann-bodied Type 44 about to embark on a rally and Concours in December 1929. The photo shows Lamberjack, a Paris Bugatti agent, and the daughter of Ernest Friderich in the Place de la Concorde, Paris.
Type 44, carrosserie Weymann avant un rallye en décembre 1929. Sur la photo Lamberjack, agent Bugatti à Paris, et la fille d'Ernest Friderich. Place de la Concorde.

A Gangloff saloon taking part in the Paris-Saint Raphaël Rallye Féminin in the winter of 1929-30.
Berline Gangloff ayant pris part, l'hiver 1929-30, au Rallye féminin Paris-Saint Raphaël.

A Type 49 Gangloff enduring a slow-running competition in Montmartre; circa 1931-32.
Type 49 Gangloff dans une course de lenteur à Montmartre vers 1931-32.

CHAPTER TEN

OBSERVATIONS ON OWNERSHIP AND USE IN BRITAIN

The buyer of a new car will have been a discerning person of considerable affluence, and will, no doubt, have been influenced by the racing successes of Bugatti, at its zenith during the production period of the Type 44.

He, or occasionally she, will also have been seduced by the appearance, particularly the distinctive radiator, making for instant recognition by the cognoscenti. Showing the exquisite under-bonnet finish and classic proportions of the power plant will also have made the salesman's job a pleasure. The buyer will have been convinced by advertising and a trial run that a Bugatti was a civilised touring car, while the precise and accurate steering will have been a source of some amazement.

The rate of depreciation, as with all comparatively rare and expensive cars, particularly of foreign manufacture, would have been very high, but probably of little importance for the first owner. The car will have served for at least eight to nine years unless subjected to accident or major mechanical disaster. 1935 would see the value for a sound car drop to seventy pounds, or even less, while this figure will have reduced to about twenty pounds by 1939. One has to take into account that the pound sterling of pre-war value has to be multiplied by a factor of sixty or seventy in order to achieve a comparison with present-day values. During the period of 1935-39 the scrappage rate will have begun to multiply, while the survivors would almost certainly have endured a total lay-up or have succumbed to the wartime drive for scrap aluminium. Survivors will have been priced at one hundred to one hundred and fifty pounds in 1946, while the low point of post-war value appears to have been 1958-59, when a good example might only have commanded fifty to seventy pounds. A gradual climb was soon to take place, though, which has accelerated to a point where we have seen several examples of this type sold for eighty to one hundred thousand pounds in the recent past.

A considerable proportion of the 'British cars' were fitted with fabric bodies, built under Weymann principles. The survival rate of this type of coachwork was comparatively low, resulting in the construction of new bodies, often by amateur coachbuilders, and likely to have been of poor quality and appearance. Several Type 43 supercharged cars were fitted with Type 44 engines in the post-war years, no doubt due to the cost of overhauling the original roller-bearing engine; a state of affairs which must have resulted in further scrappage of the three-litre car.

KNOWN SURVIVING CARS (2007)

Type	Production	Survivors
Type 30	600	32
Type 38	385	42
Type 44	1095	165
Type 49	470	103

SECOND HAND PRICES

In 1927, Mrs Junek paid only 35,000F for the Type 38 chassis (38585) which, with a Loiseau Type 40 Sahara

A Van Vooren fabric saloon built under Weymann patents. We have seen an identical body on a Ballot; note the heavily grained fabric.
Limousine de Van Vooren sous licence Weymann. La même carrosserie a été réalisée pour une Ballot; on peut remarquer le grain épais du simili-cuir.

coachwork, had been used as a service car in the Targa Florio.

After the 1929-1930 Depression, second hand cars became very difficult to sell. Some models, like the Types 30 or 38 disappeared from the small ads of the British owners' club bulletin; prices for the 44 between 1932 and 1938 vary from £95 to £325, and for the 49 from £190 to £285.

Below: A similar car imported to England and used as a road test car and considered to be chassis number 44305. The picture was taken outside St James' Park, London W1.
Une voiture semblable importée en l'Angleterre et utilisée comme voiture de démonstration. Le numéro de chassis pourrait être 44305; photo prise près de St. James' Park à Londres.

Type 44. A genuine Weymann built by Weymann's English factory in Addlestone, Surrey.
Une carrosserie Weymann construite dans l'usine anglaise à Addlestone (Surrey).

Type 44. A coupé by Harrington of Hove under Weymann licence.
Coupé Harrington de Hove sous licence Weymann.

Another Harrington coupé, chassis number 44787, which survives in perfect original condition.
Chassis numéro 44787 carrossé par Harrington et en parfait état d'origine.

Interior of chassis 44787. Note the high quality of veneer and woodwork.
Chassis 44787. remarquer la très bonne qualité de la marqueterie.

Chassis number 49492; bodied by the English coachbuilder James Young of Bromley.
Chassis numéro 49492 de James Young de Bromley.

Two more bodies by the English coachbuilder James Young of Bromley:
chassis number 49512 (above); photographed at Prescott, UK.
Deux carrosseries anglaises de James Young de Bromley. Chassis numéro 49512 (ci-dessus) photographié à Prescott.

Chassis number 49513; note the raked windscreen and separate side lights on this car.
Chassis numéro 49513. Remarquer le pare-brise incliné et les feux de position.

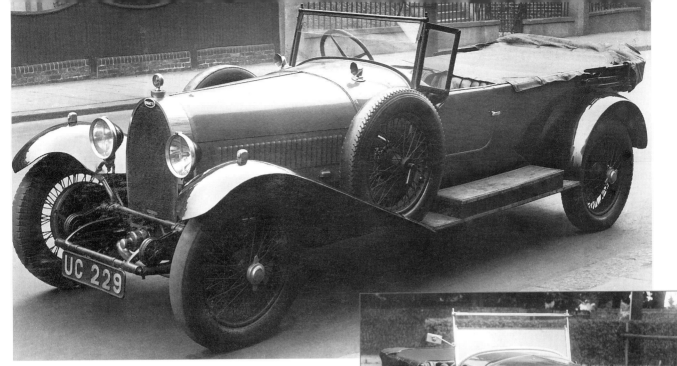

A tourer by Compton of Hanworth. There is no rear door to the near-side, and note 'ship fog horn' ventilators to assist cooling the feet, a popular British accessory at the time. Chassis number 44267.

Chassis numéro 44267 carrossé par Compton de Hanworth. Pas de porte arrière, à gauche; remarquer les entrées de ventilation en forme de cornes de brume, accessoire anglais courant à cette époque.

A Jarvis-bodied car, later the property of Sir Ralph Millais, grandson of the famous painter.
Carrosserie Jarvis achetée plus tard par Sir Ralph Millais, petit-fils du célèbre peintre.

Another Jarvis car, photographed in later life; wing lines spoilt. Chassis number 44722.
Chassis numéro 44722 carrossé par Jarvis; voiture modifiée avec un dessin d'ailes peu réussi.

Chassis number 441225. Fabric body by Harrington of Hove; note the unusual split-rimmed wheels. This car survives in original condition.
Chassis numéro 441225 carrossé par Harrington à Hove. Remarquer les jantes des roues. Cette voiture a été conservée

This car was supplied by the London depot to Captain J F C Kruse, who commissioned royal coachbuilder Hooper to build this touring body, completed in 1930 and thus a Type 44. Registered in London, GH 3730, chassis number unknown, this car has not been traced.
Voiture vendue par l'agence de Londres au Capitaine J F C Kruse qui fit réaliser en 1930 par Hooper (carrossier de la Cour britannique), ce torpédo de Type 44 immatriculé GH 3730 à Londres; le numéro de chassis n'est pas connu et la voiture a disparu.

A Type 49 4-seater tourer by Corsica of Edgware Road, London, built on chassis number 49118. Originally ordered by Bugatti Club President, Colonel Goff Giles.

Chassis numéro 49118 carrossé par Corsica (Edgware Road à Londres), commandé par le Président du Club Bugatti anglais, le Colonel Goff Giles.

The above car competing at Prescott in the early post-war years, driven by Mrs Peter Clark.
La même voiture en course de côte à Prescott conduite après la guerre par Mme Peter Clark.

A Type 30 by Jarvis of Wimbledon. Note the aluminium bonnet.
Type 30 carrossée par Jarvis de Wimbledon. Remarquer le capot bouchonné.

Chassis number 49500 imported to England and fitted with coachwork by Corsica/Jarvis. Originally used as a trials car and subjected to a full Autocar road test. Owned by Peter Wilks, technical director of the Rover Company in the early post-war years, it still exists in original condition.
Chassis numéro 49500 exporté en Grande-Bretagne pour être carrossé par Corsica/Jarvis. Utilisée à l'origine comme voiture de démonstration, elle fut l'objet d'un essai complet paru dans la célèbre revue Autocar. Propriété de Peter Wilks, directeur technique de Rover après la guerre, la voiture existe toujours dans son état d'origine.

The same car with the hood erected.
La même voiture capotée.

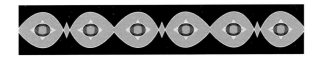

The first Type 49 to be owned by the Giles family and bodied by Compton of Hanworth in Middlesex in the style of a Type 43 Grand Sport. Two or three similar examples were built.

La première 49 de la famille Giles, carrossée par Compton de Hanworth dans le style d'un Type 43 Grand Sport. Deux ou trois exemplaires ont été construits.

CHAPTER ELEVEN

DRIVING BUGATTIS IN THE THIRTIES

Even if Bugatti was publishing advertisements saying that his cars "did not wear out", a driver's life was not always easy. Looking at the list of weekly maintenance required, it was only really Sunday that was considered a rest day!

There were many mechanical items that required regular attention: valves and pistons had to be decoked after 10,000 or 15,000 kilometres, and clutch discs had to be oiled, adjusted or changed. Tyres had a rather short life, even in countries where metalled roads were the rule; but many roads in Europe were unmade. Punctures were

A holiday at Puy en Velay, Massif Central. Chassis number 49135 and a Type 44.
Promenade de vacances au Puy en Velay (Massif Central). Chassis numéro 49135 et un Type 44.

frequent and, for this reason, many Bugattis and other large cars, such as the Delage, Hispano or Mercedes, carried two spare wheels, and even extra tyres.

Bugatti was delivering the Types 44 and 49 with twenty tools, a syringe for the clutch, a grease gun, and numerous instruction booklets for carburettor, electric circuit and battery. The owner was clearly expected to use those tools frequently!

On early Types 30 and 38 the coachwork was often spartan: bodies were narrow, often without a hood or space for extensive luggage.

Bad weather was a nightmare, even if far-sighted owners had special raincoats, which the French called 'parapluies de chauffeurs' (umbrellas for chauffeurs). For these reasons cars were used only locally, and many were left in the garage during the winter. Later, bodies giving better protection were built, but the weight on Types 30 and 38 was often too high and performance and reliability suffered. In Britain, where roads were very good, drivers were using their cars more extensively: 51,000km (31,000 miles) for a Type 44 over a three year period, and 33,000km (20,300 miles) in 16 months for a Type 49, claimed proud owners in the Bugatti Owners' Club magazine.

In Europe, roads gradually improved, tyres became safer, and cars could be used for longer journeys. Nevertheless, a trip from England to Paris and Chantilly with a Type 49 was considered a real feat, worth several pages in an April 1938 *Bulletin*.

On the continent, where driving long distances was the norm, travelling from Paris to Nice (950km), for example, or Berlin-Munich (550km) would have taken several days at an average speed of between 50-70kph.

Owners who had a chauffeur would usually take the train, with family and luggage. Boots were very small, and the chauffeur would drive the car alone. To cross a European boundary one had to show a Carnet de passage en douane, which needed to be affiliated to an Automobile Club. Customs officers checked chassis and engine number, and sometimes duties had to be paid on the petrol in the tank! Cars also had to carry a nationality plate at the rear.

As every passport was stamped and often each piece of luggage inspected, half an hour or more at Customs was a

A Type 38 behind a Type 40, on holiday in France during the summer of 1958.
Un Type 38 devant un Type 40, sur la route des vacances en 1958.

normal delay. Mountain passes were a particular nightmare: roads were bad and narrow, with difficult hairpin bends. It was impossible to pass a lorry or a slower car, and some passes, like the Galibier in France, allowed only one car at a time, and descending cars had to wait at a 'refuge'. In the summer, boiling radiators were a common sight, with passengers waiting in the sun while the driver went on foot to find some water!

Because they had four gears, a water pump and a

Crossing the channel in the thirties. A 1931 Type 44 Coach, chassis number 441158, is hoisted aboard the channel ferry; we think the Boulogne-Folkestone route. The owner is on deck giving instructions.
Dans un port de la Manche, Gangloff 441158 est embarquée. Sur le pont, le propriétaire donne des indications.

good quality radiator, Bugattis fared better in mountains than many cars. Cars with three gears and without water pumps heated inexorably, as did many lorries that were often overloaded. There were other hazards; road workers who could not at this time afford a car hated owners of big cars and their chauffeurs; when the road was up, they often did their best to block the path or to put down too much tar, which was not good for the coachwork.

Crossing by sea was another difficulty as cars had to be hoisted onto the boats by crane, and often stayed on the deck under tarpaulins. These trips did little to improve the cars. Luckily, more care was taken when cars like Bugattis were exported to far flung countries, such as Australia, New Zealand, the United States or Argentina.

By Jean-Louis Arbey

CHAPTER TWELVE

OWNERS MANUALS AND PARTS CATALOGUES

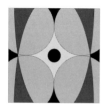

Bugatti supplied owners of the Type 30 with a rudimentary manual; 15 pages, of modest size, (3.7 x 8.3 inches or 145 x 210mm), without any pictures. Printed by Josst at Mutzig, a small town near Molsheim, this manual listed a frightful number of figures! For instance, the maximum weight of the petrol for one litre and a long list of recommendations.

Oiling and greasing, every 100, 500, 1500 kilometres (930 miles) was covered in detail, as were the use and quality of rags, and the wire material to be used to clear an oil jet. The gearbox and rear axle had to be attended to every month and, curiously, the gearbox had to receive thick oil and grease.

Instructions on valve grinding and decarbonising, best left to a mechanic, were included, but the motor's description covered how you could assemble the crankshaft and its ball bearings, without any hint of giving such work to a 'knowledgeable person' ... or, as written in French, 'une personne très au courant.'

Engine lubrication was briefly described as being by pump and splash. The word used was a 'noble force centrifuge' and not the usual 'barbotage'! Some spelling mistakes could be found in this manual and, for the clutch, the use of 'lamelle' for discs, which is a German word.

The Type 40 and Type 38 handbook, common to both models, was a much better publication, and quite different. Thirty eight pages (8.3 x 10.6 inches 210 x 270mm) printed on a very good paper, with drawings and forty two well retouched pictures. Its legibility was helped by the use of red figures. Advice was given about running in, no more than 2500rpm for the first 2000km (1240 miles), and the text was more succinct than that in the Type 30 manual. Nevertheless, two pages were given over to adjusting the valve clearances.

The Type 44 and Type 49 manuals were also 3.7 x 8.3 inches. There were twenty three pictures comprehensively detailing maintaining the engine, clutch, brakes, and so forth, but the sentence used in the Type 40 manual "... the successive improvements on cars have reduced the maintenance to an extreme simplicity ... " is omitted!

The running in period was reduced to 1000 kilometres and 100kmh, though the rpm limit was not stated as many cars were built without rev-counters.

The final page listed twenty five tools, and sentences were included covering electrics, battery, and carburettors. Bugatti helped further with special pages about plugs, oils and jet sizes. A starting handle was in the set of tools, nothing was said about the danger of backfire kick, and there was no instruction about jacking up.

The Type 49 manual was similar, but described some particularities. A sleeve on the gearlever for selecting reverse, for example, the foot switch for dipping the lights, and the three position ignition key (one position commanding all 16 plugs, and both sets separately), seen previously on the Royale and Type 46.

In August 1930, Bugatti published a forty two page parts catalogue (8.3 x 10.6 inches) for the Type 44. Twenty three pages were given over to the seven hundred and sixty three separate parts, and fifteen pages were for illustrations. A very clear catalogue with a thick cover, it was well printed and was presented as for the Types 40 and 38 manuals. We do not believe that another Type received such a comprehensive volume.

By Jean-Louis Arbey

A selection of typical parts catalogues.

Une sélection des catalogues typiques des pièces de rechange.

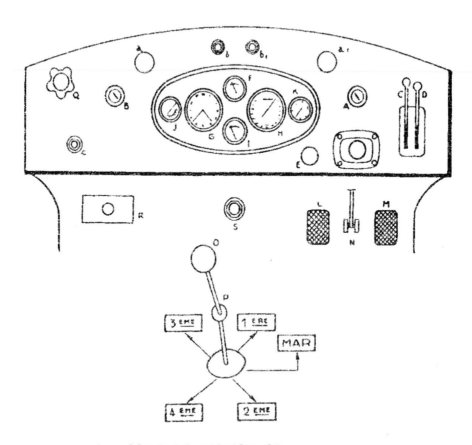

A — CONTACT D'ALLUMAGE
B — CONTACT D'ÉCLAIRAGE
C — MANETTE D'AVANCE
D — MANETTE DE GAZ
E — TIRETTE DE DÉPART
F — AMPÈREMÈTRE
G — MONTRE
H — COMPTEUR KILOMÉTRIQUE
I — MANOMÈTRE D'HUILE
J — INDICATEUR D'ESSENCE
K — THERMOMÈTRE
L — PÉDALE DE DÉBRAYAGE
M — PÉDALE DE FREIN
N — PÉDALE D'ACCÉLÉRATEUR
O — LEVIER DE VITESSE
P — BAGUE DE MARCHE AR.
Q — BOUTON DE RÉGLAGE D'AMORTISSEURS
R — BOITE A FUSIBLES
S — BOUTON DE CODE AU PIED

a a¹ - Lampes de bord
b   - Bouton des lampes de bord
b¹   - Bouton d'éclairage intérieur
c   - Bouton de jauge d'essence

PRÉCAUTIONS HEBDOMADAIRES

LUNDI

Vérifier la pression des pneus AV   2 kgs, AR   2,250 kgs

MARDI

Graisser les articulations des ressorts AV et AR et celles de la direction. Graisser les axes de fusée.

MERCREDI

Vérifier le niveau d'eau de la batterie d'Accumulateurs. Graisser les articulations de cardans.

JEUDI

Démonter le filtre à huile et le nettoyer (de préférence avec du benzol en se servant d'un pinceau dur). Vérifier le niveau d'huile du carter moteur. Compléter avec l'huile **BUGATTI CS**

VENDREDI

Nettoyer l'embrayage au pétrole. Refaire le plein avec le mélange   Pétrole $^1/_3$ Huile BUGATTI T. Vérifier et graisser l'arbre du pédalier. Vérifier les câbles de frein. Graisser les pignons de chaîne.

SAMEDI

Vérifier le distributeur d'allumage. Vérifier la pompe à essence. Vérifier le graisseur de pompe à eau (Graisse Bugatti spéciale).

HUILES BUGATTI

Les **HUILES BUGATTI** sont en vente chez tous les agents de la marque ainsi que dans les principaux garages.

CHAPTER THIRTEEN

FIACRES

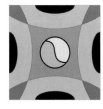

Ettore Bugatti had a lifelong love of animals and always owned a horse. In later years he built a stagecoach with which he intended to cross the Alps to visit his birthplace in Milan, but the carriage was never completed. In later years, Bugatti built a stagecoach with which he intended to cross the Alps, Hannibal fashion, but this carriage was never totally finished.

Bugatti had several versions of the Fiacre style built, which translates to Hansom Cab in English, and these clearly show their horse-drawn origins.

By Barrie Price

This page & opposite: Considered the first two Fiacres built, photographed in the winter of 1927-28. Note the Grand Prix Type radiator thermometer on one car finished all black, while the second car has a two-tone paint scheme, unless it is the same car repainted and with thermometer removed.

Considérées comme étant les deux premières voitures du Type Fiacre, elles ont été photographiées pendant l'hiver 1927-28. Remarquer le thermomètre du radiateur de Type Grand Prix sur la voiture peinte en noir, alors que l'autre est peinte en deux tons; peut-être s'agit de la même voiture repeinte et sans thermomètre.

One picture was taken in the factory grounds facing the Bugatti house; note the conservatory built by Ettore.
Photo prise sur les terrains de l'usine située en face de la maison de la famille Bugatti: remarquer le jardin d'hiver construit par Bugatti..

Jean Bugatti with a Fiacre.
Jean Bugatti à côté d'un Fiacre.

Another version photographed outside the Bugatti chateau; note the opening doors in the bonnet side instead of louvres. Again, possibly the first car, yet again modified. We are inclined to this view.

Autre Fiacre photographié devant le château Saint-Jean. Noter sur le capot les trappes d'aération à la place des fentes; il pourrait s'agir de la première voiture, modifiée une fois de plus.

A similar style, now without wheel discs and fitted with proprietary double row bumpers, which was the latest fashion accessory and a convenient perch for a youthful Jean Bugatti in up-to-the-minute Plus-Fours!

Voiture de même style, mais sans enjoliveurs avec pare-chocs double à la dernière mode sur lequel est assis Jean Bugatti, en pantalons de golf très à la mode en France à cette époque.

Recent pictures of two surviving Fiacres; note the differing wing lines. The car with door draught excluders is pictured with its owner, the late Alan Sodorstrom.

Photos récentes de deux Fiacres qui existent encore; remarquer les différences de ligne des ailes et les déflecteurs. La photo est prise avec Alan Sodorstrom, aujourd'hui décédé.

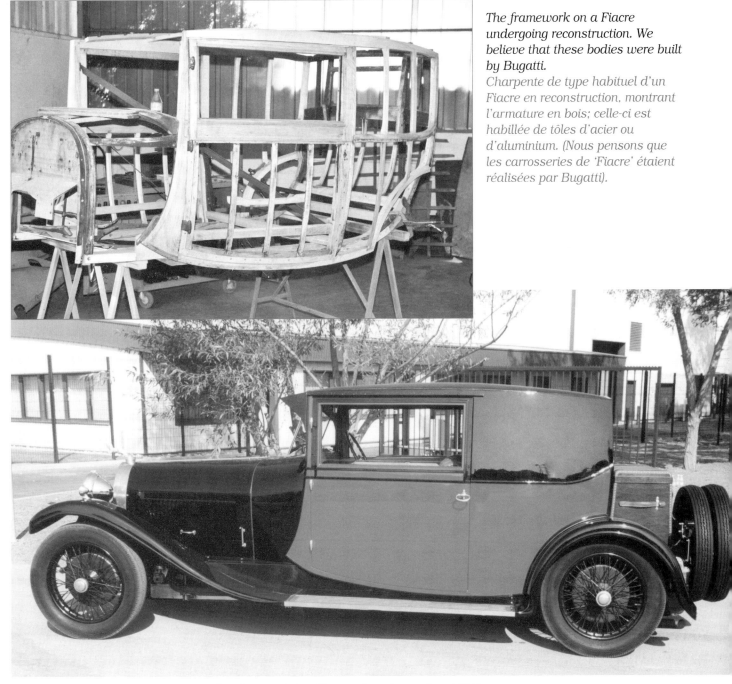

The framework on a Fiacre undergoing reconstruction. We believe that these bodies were built by Bugatti.
Charpente de type habituel d'un Fiacre en reconstruction, montrant l'armature en bois; celle-ci est habillée de tôles d'acier ou d'aluminium. (Nous pensons que les carrosseries de 'Fiacre' étaient réalisées par Bugatti).

Another surviving Fiacre, chassis number 44541.
Autre Fiacre existant; numéro de chassis 44541.

A 'total' Fiacre two-seater version; note the horse carriage rocker panel.

Fiacre en version deux places. Remarquer le dessin de la caisse.

Another two-seater version with standard dickey-seat instead of luggage trunk. Mlle Hellé-Nice in front appears to have been careless, judging by the damaged wings.

Autre version deux places avec sièges additionnels à la place de la malle arrière. Il semble que la conductrice – Mlle Hellé-Nice – a endommagé une aile.

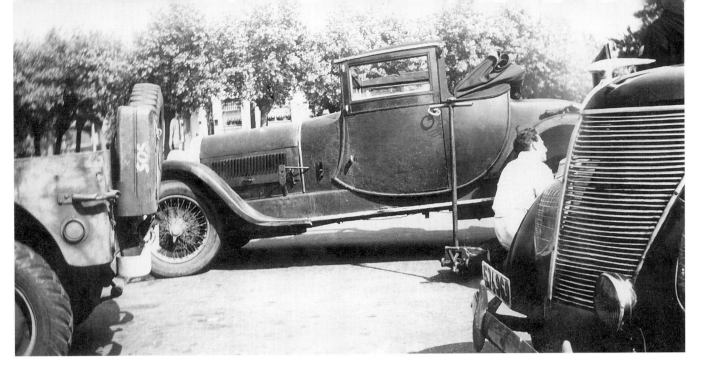

A rare drophead version of a two-seater Fiacre, chassis number 441192, photographed in Belgium in the early post-war years when in the ownership of a Catholic priest. Unfortunately, the car was later scrapped.

Une rare version décapotable d'un Fiacre deux places numéro 441192. Photo faite en Belgique peu après cette guerre quand elle appartenait à un prêtre catholique; voiture détruite depuis.

Fiacre on a Type 44, with 49 wheels. Chassis number 44580. Photographed in the workshop of Henri Novo in the post-war years; note the second series Type 57 Galibier in the background.

Fiacre 44 avec des roues de 49. Chassis numéro 44580. La voiture qui existe toujours a été photographiée dans l'atelier d' Henri Novo après cette guerre; au fond une 57 Galibier, deuxième série.

CHAPTER FOURTEEN

FIXED HEAD COUPÉS

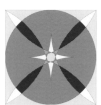

This style enjoyed a vogue during the late twenties and early thirties. Alought often extremely elegant, the passengers in the rear of these (mostly) four seaters did not enjoy good visibility.

These bodies were often of composite design: fabric top, metal panels below.

Chassis number 44375 with a body by Gangloff; at left the owner Guillaume Prick, founder of the Dutch Bugatti Club.
Chassis numéro 44375 carrossé par Gangloff; à gauche le propriétaire Guillaume Prick, fondateur du Bugatti Club néerlandais.

A well-known and stylish body by D'Ieteren Frères of Brussels on chassis number 44637.

Chassis numéro 44637 avec une carrosserie très connue et de bon style réalisée par d'Ieteren Frères à Bruxelles.

A genuine Weymann coupé photographed outside the Bugatti agency in Marseille.

Coupé Weymann photographié devant l'agence Bugatti de Marseille.

A close-coupled fixed head Type 44; chassis number unknown.
Type 44 – numéro de chassis inconnu pour ce faux cabriolet.

A stylish fixed-head coupé on chassis number 441119, nowadays resident in Sweden.
Chassis numéro 441119. Coupé d'un excellent dessin appartenant à un Suédois.

Chassis 49210, a fixed-head coupé by Czech builder Uhlik. This car survives in the Mulhouse Museum.
Chassis numéro 49210. Faux cabriolet carrossé par Uhlik (Prague), se trouvant au Musée de Mulhouse.

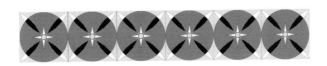

CHAPTER FIFTEEN

SALOONS (BERLINES)

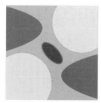

The four door saloon, invariably in close coupled (Four Light) style, was popular on all sporting chassis in the pre-war period. These were often in composite form, fabric covered above the waistline and metal panelled below, and generally fitted with a luggage trunk at the rear, often detachable.

The standard Berline designed by Bugatti and built by Gangloff. This is an original publicity picture taken inside the factory grounds with the family garden behind. The upper quarters of this car are fabric covered, but the panelled doors are metal.

Berline standard dessinée par Bugatti et construite par Gangloff. Photo de publicité réalisée sur le terrain de l'usine; le jardin familial est au second plan. Le toit de la voiture est recouvert de tissu mais les portes sont en métal.

A four-light saloon, believed Van Vooren and possibly early Type 49, with plated window frames and a fabric top; note the long, multi-louvred bonnet and the Marchal foglights.

Berline avec des entourages de glaces chromés et un toit en tissue. Construite sans doute par Van Vooren. Remarquer le capot à fentes multiples et les phares de brouillard Marchal. Ce pourrait être une 49 de début de série.

Chassis number 49318, the work of Sodomka of Prague.

Chassis numéro 49318, carrosserie de Sodomka de Prague.

A late Type 49 with heavy coachwork by Erdmann et Rossi of Berlin, and Zeiss headlamps. There are no running boards on this car.

Type 49 de fin de série avec une carrosserie faite par Erdmann et Rossi de Berlin. Remarquer les phares Zeiss et l'absence de marchepied.

A late four-door saloon, coachbuilder unknown, with
trailing doors.
*Berline de fin de série, carrossier inconnu,
portes à charnières avant.*

Right: The dashboard of a Type 49 with adjustable shock absorbers
by Dufaux-Repusseau; note the original Bugatti coachwork plaque.
*Tableau de bord d'un Type 49 avec amortisseurs réglables Dufaux-
Repusseau. Remarquer la plaque de carrosserie Bugatti d'origine.*

The interior of chassis number 49362, a Van Vooren saloon in totally original condition. This car had separate shock
absorber controls from front and rear, central accelerator and a foot-operated headlamp dip-switch.
*Intérieur d'une limousine Van Vooren (Chassis numéro 49362) en état d'origine. Remarquer les commandes
d'amortisseurs réglables pour l'avant et l'arrière, l'accélérateur central et la commande de phares au pied.*

Chassis number 441179, a neat four-light saloon by d'Allain et Lieutard.
Chassis numéro 441179, berline de dessin classique carrosserie d'Allain et Lieutard.

Chassis 49450, a late series saloon by Ruckstuhl of Switzerland, with forward opening doors.
Berline Ruckstuhl (Suisse) de fin de série avec 4 portes ouvrant vers l'avant. Chassis 49450.

CHAPTER SIXTEEN

TWO·DOOR SALOONS (COACHES)

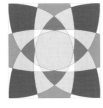

An alternative saloon version. Access to the rear seats with this type was awkward, and involved the necessity of a folding front seat squab similar to those found in the coupés. Nevertheless, this was a bestselling style on later cars.

This page & overleaf: Three factory shots of the catalogue Type 44 two-door saloon with fabric top. The stylised shot shows a Fiacre in motion. Chassis number 44882.
Trois reproductions du catalogue du Type 44 montrant un coupé. Remarquer le toit en simili-cuir et le dessin montrant un 'Fiacre' en vitesse. Sans doute chassis 44882.

A Type 49 by Van Vooren, for many years in the ownership of racing driver Jules Goux; chassis number 49414.
Type 49 carrossée par Van Vooren (chassis numéro 49414) ayant appartenu pendant longtemps au coureur Jules Goux.

Another Van Vooren, chassis number 49362, but with fabric top and more curvaceous roof and waistline.
Autre Van Vooren, chassis numéro 49362, avec un toit en simili-cuir et une caisse aux courbes accentuées.

A rare picture of Prince Lobkowitz, taken probably only hours before his death in a Type 54 Grand Prix car at Avus, Berlin. Careful study reveals a factory-bodied Type 49 fixed-head coupé with a strange sliding door arrangement, a scheme tried by other coachbuilders at this period; clearly a special sample body. The Art Deco stoneguard, proprietary front bumper, and weird side lamps were presumably ordered by Lobkowitz.

Une photo rare du Prince Lobkowitz prise sans doute quelques heures avant sa mort sur un Type 54 Grand

Prix au circuit de l'Avus près de Berlin. Un examen attentif de la photo montre qu'il s'agit d'un coupé Type 49 avec une porte montée sur rail; d'autres carrossiers, à cette époque, adoptèrent ce système. Le pare-pierres de style Art déco, le pare-chocs spécial et les curieux feux de position avaient sans doute été commandées spécialement par Lobkowitz.

A strange two-door saloon Type 44. Special features include a full length bonnet with multi-angled louvres containing the Bugatti emblem; a special cover over the twin rear wheels; slats protecting the petrol tank; and a thin chromium frame around the door which, presumably, drops with the glass. This car would appear to have a polished aluminium finish; chassis number unknown.

Une limousine Type 44 deux portes (numéro de

chassis inconnu) d'un dessin très particulier. Le capot a de nombreuses fentes et un logo Bugatti de grande dimension. Les roues de secours sont bâchées, le réservoir est protégé et les vitres des portes sont entourées par une partie chromée. Il semble que cette voiture ait été en aluminium poli.

A semi-profilée body by Bugatti on chassis number 49551.
Chassis numéro 49551. Voiture semi-profilée carrossée par Bugatti.

A similar body on chassis number 44784, which must have been fitted at a later date; the front wings would have been designed by Jean Bugatti.
Chassis 44784, cette carrosserie semblable à celle du haut a remplacé la carrosserie d'origine. Remarquer les ailes avant dessinées par Jean Bugatti.

A body by Tomas of Prague on chassis number 441331, almost the last Type 44. This photograph was taken in Prague in the 1950s.

Chassis numéro 441331 un des derniers du Type 44. Carrosserie Tomas de Prague. La voiture existe toujours; photo prise à Prague après cette guerre.

Chassis number 49320, a close coupled style by Ludwig.

Chassis numéro 49320 un cabriolet représentatif du style de Ludwig.

A futuristic pillarless saloon of a late Type 49 by Labourdette with wire wheels. Chassis number unknown. Barrie Price considers it conceivable that the lower picture could be the same car re-profiled in later life.

Deux 49 de fin de série par Labourdette. Numéros de chassis inconnus. Coupés sans montant central. La voiture (en haut) a un dessin très novateur pour l'époque.

CHAPTER SEVENTEEN

CABRIOLETS

This type was popular in the thirties, particularly on expensive chassis. They were never as satisfactory as a saloon due to the lack of rigidity, heavy doors, and a tendency to rattle and squeak when aged.

A very early Type 49, chassis number 49534. The coachwork, by Labourdette, has been heavily modernised at a later date.
Type 49 numéro 49534, de début de série; carrosserie Labourdette, très modernisée ultérieurement.

A Gaston Grummer cabriolet which appears to be fabric covered; note the split-rimmed wheels.

Cabriolet Gaston Grummer; carrosserie recouverte de simili-cuir. Remarquer la fente des jantes.

The stand of Ernest Friderich at the Nice Motor Show, 1928. There is a saloon Type 44 in left background, with an attractive Bugatti-designed, American-influenced, and built by Gangloff, two-seater in the right foreground. Matched by Grand Sport Type 40 and the miniature Type 52 on a table.

Stand d'Ernest Friderich au Salon automobile de Nice en 1928. A l'arrière-plan une berline Type 44 à droite, d'après un dessin de Bugatti, d'influence américaine un cabriolet deux-places de Gangloff.

De l'autre côté un Type 40 Grand sport et sur la table une 52, voiture électrique pour enfants.

*Chassis number 44518,
rebodied in late 1930s style;
considered Gangloff.
Type 44 numéro 44518,
recarrossé dans le style des
années 30, à peu près sûrement
par Gangloff.*

*Chassis number 441261, very
late coupé by Letourneur et
Marchand embodying special
features for use in Tunisia.
Ugly hood when furled.
Type 44 numéro 441261, coupé
Letourneur et Marchand, avec
capot spécial pour la Tunisie.
Repliée, la capote est trop
apparente.*

Chassis number 44942, a Type 44 coupé by Lavocat et Marsaud.
Type 44 numéro 44942. Coupé Lavocat et Marsaud.

Type 44, chassis number 44692, Gangloff body, discovered in the 1990s.
Type 44 numéro 44692 par Gangloff, retrouvée dans les années 90.

Believed to be chassis number 441088, a strange coupé; note Fiacre-style scuttle line. Probably the work of Sodomka of Prague. Another car with a radiator stoneguard.
Sans doute chassis 441088; coupé inhabituel réalisé probablement par Sodomka de Prague avec une grille de protection pour le radiateur.

Type 44, chassis number 441074, coachbuilder
Reufflet; note carriage handles.
*Type 44 numéro 441074; carrossé par Reufflet.
Remarquer les poignées rondes.*

Type 44, chassis number 441092, photographed in
early post-war years, unfortunately scrapped some
time later; coachbuilder unknown.
*Type 44 numéro 441092 photographié dans les
années 50, carrossier inconnu; voiture détruite.*

Believed to be chassis number 44675, by Marcel Proux of Paris.
Sans doute chassis numéro 44675. Carrosserie Marcel Proux de Paris.

Chassis number 49566 by Gangloff.
Type 49 numéro 49566 carrosserie Gangloff.

Opposite: Chassis 49248, coachbuilder Chiattone of Lugano, in front of another 49, the latter re-bodied in the style of a Jean Bugatti roadster. Photograph taken in 2002, Rallye des Marques.

Ci-contre: Chassis numéro 49248, carrosserie par Chiattone de Lugano, devant une autre 49, recarrossée dans le style d'un roadster Jean Bugatti. Photo prise en 2002 au Rallye des Marques.

Another drophead coupé, chassis number 49570 by Van Rijswijk (The Hague), but conceivably intended for a different chassis to judge by the awkward bonnet/scuttle line.

Coupé décapotable par Van Rijswijk (La Haye), chassis numéro 49570; le dessin médiocre laisse à penser que la carrosserie vient du chassis d'une autre marque.

107

A late drophead, the work of Swiss coachbuilder Graber.
Réalisation du carrossier suisse Graber.

Another coupé in arctic conditions; coachbuilder unknown.
Autre coupé dans le Nord de l'Europe. Carrossier inconnu.

Type 49, chassis number 49227, a coupé by Sodomka of Prague but in the Gangloff idiom. Note the radiator stoneguard.

Type 49 numéro 49227 par Sodomka de Prague comparable aux carrosseries de Gangloff. Noter la grille de protection du radiateur.

Another coupé considered the work of Graber; note the full length, many-louvred bonnet.
Autre coupé attribué à Graber. Noter les nombreuses fentes du capot.

Chassis number 49172, a surviving car now in Mulhouse Museum; coachwork by Tomas of Prague.
Type 49 numéro 49172, carrossé par Tomas de Prague. Exposé au Musée de Mulhouse.

CHAPTER EIGHTEEN

ROADSTERS AND SPORTS CARS

The popularity of light, two-seater bodies declined in the thirties, because they relied on often ill-fitting celluloid side screens for weather protection. These styles were largely displaced by the heavier drop-head coupé, which was normally draught-proof.

Elizabeth Junek on her Indian tour in a Bugatti-designed, Gangloff-built roadster. She sold the car for Ettore before returning home.
Elisabeth Junek au cours de son voyage aux Indes avec un roadster carrossé par Gangloff sur un dessin Bugatti. Elle vendit la voiture pour Ettore avant son retour à Prague.

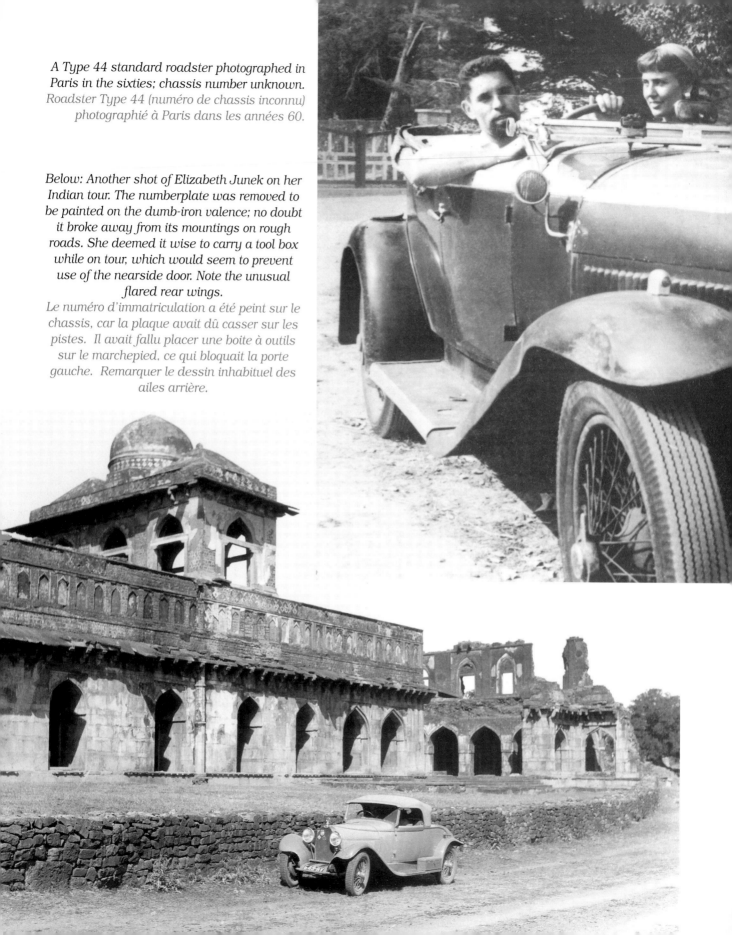

A Type 44 standard roadster photographed in Paris in the sixties; chassis number unknown.
Roadster Type 44 (numéro de chassis inconnu) photographié à Paris dans les années 60.

Below: Another shot of Elizabeth Junek on her Indian tour. The numberplate was removed to be painted on the dumb-iron valence; no doubt it broke away from its mountings on rough roads. She deemed it wise to carry a tool box while on tour, which would seem to prevent use of the nearside door. Note the unusual flared rear wings.
Le numéro d'immatriculation a été peint sur le chassis, car la plaque avait dû casser sur les pistes. Il avait fallu placer une boite à outils sur le marchepied, ce qui bloquait la porte gauche. Remarquer le dessin inhabituel des ailes arrière.

Chassis number 441063, standard Bugatti body, similar to Type 40A with golf club locker.
Chassis numéro 441063 avec une carrosserie de Type 40A; remarquer la trappe pour clubs de golf.

Chassis number 441336, a late Type 44, copying the Bugatti line but built by de Villars.
Chassis numéro 441336 de fin de série inspiré de Bugatti et carrossé par de Villars.

Chassis number 441216, a standard roadster, still in existence in the USA.
Chassis numéro 441216, roadster classique; aux Etats-Unis.

Another American-owned car; chassis number 44572.
Autre voiture exportée aux Etats-Unis, chassis numéro 44572.

Gangloff-built car, Bugatti-styled wings. The windscreen is typically French and, no doubt, the work of a specialist firm.
Voiture carrossée par Gangloff, ailes de style Bugatti et pare-brise spécial d'origine française.

Chassis number 441263, another standard roadster with special windscreen arrangement.
Chassis numéro 441263 autre roadster classique avec un pare-brise spécial.

Chassis number 441235. A 1930 model modified for the 1936 Le Mans race which was cancelled due to industrial action in France. Frame shortened, engine, transmission and brakes all modified: in the USA since 1952.
Chassis numéro 441235 de 1930 modifié pour les 24 heures du Mans de 1936 qui furent annulées à cause des grèves. Chassis raccourci, moteur, freins et transmission modifiés; aux Etats-Unis depuis 1952.

A roadster in the Gangloff style but built after the war by the little known coachbuilder, Pichon-Parat of Sens. (Type 49.)
Roadster de style Gangloff (Type 49) réalisé après la guerre par un carrossier de Sens. Pichon-Parat.

New coachwork in the Gangloff style.
Carrosserie récente de style Gangloff.

A well-executed replica incorporating Jean Bugatti wing line; chassis number 49572.
Chassis numéro 49572. Copie de carrosserie de bonne facture avec utilisation du dessin d'ailes de Jean Bugatti.

A flamboyant roadster, the work of Gläser on chassis number 49421.
Chassis numéro 49421, roadster carrossé par Gläser.

A Type 49 roadster emerging from storage; chassis number 49534.
Roadster de Type 49 sorti de grange. Chassis numéro 49534.

Both photographs show replica coachwork on a Type 44, chassis number unknown.
Chassis de numéro inconnu. Copie d'une carrosserie de Type 44.

Chassis number 49534, a late Type 49 with striking roadster body by Henri Labourdette.
Chassis numéro 49534 avec une remarquable carrosserie roadster de Labourdette.

Considered to be a replica body despite the Bugatti coachbuilder plate.
Bien qu'il y ait une plaque de carrosserie Bugatti, il s'agit sans doute d'une construction récente.

CHAPTER NINETEEN

TOURING CARS

The four-door, four-seater Touring body was the most popular style from Edwardian days until the late twenties. When cars became more powerful, allowing an increase in weight, sales of this type dropped off. The cars were also prone to rattles and draughts, and furling and erecting the long hood was a nuisance.

Chassis number 441056, a late factory-bodied tourer. This car suffered an accident in Paris in the post-war years and was transported to the Molsheim factory. Repairs did not proceed and the car remained in the works for many years until sold to the late Hugh Conway. Unfortunately, by then, the engine was missing and a replacement had to be found.

Chassis numéro 441056; cette voiture avec carrosserie d'usine fut envoyée à Molsheim après un accident à Paris dans les années 50. La voiture ne fut pas réparée et resta à l'usine avant d'être vendue à Hugh Conway senior. Le moteur d'origine, disparu, fut remplacé.

The fully-restored car is still in constant use by Hugh Conway's son.
Complètement restaurée cette voiture est couramment utilisée par le fils Conway.

A Bugatti touring car photographed in Sri Lanka, which, we believe, was the result of a sale secured by Elizabeth Junek.
Probably chassis number 44595.
Bugatti photographiée à Ceylan où Elisabeth Junek l'avait vendue. Sans doute chassis 44595.

A Gangloff-built touring car to Bugatti design showing similarity to chassis 441056. We believe the photograph was taken in the Colmar Railway goods yard.

Carrosserie de Gangloff d'un dessin semblable à la voiture 441056; photographie prise sans doute près de la gare de Colmar.

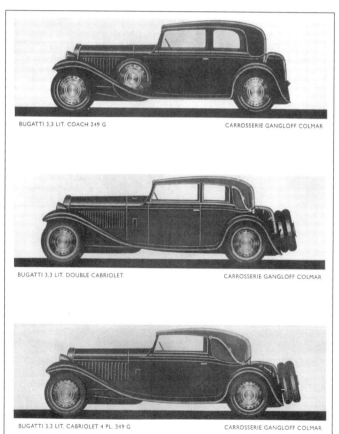

BUGATTI 3.3 LIT. COACH 249 G — CARROSSERIE GANGLOFF COLMAR

BUGATTI 3.3 LIT. DOUBLE CABRIOLET — CARROSSERIE GANGLOFF COLMAR

BUGATTI 3.3 LIT. CABRIOLET 4 PL. 349 G — CARROSSERIE GANGLOFF COLMAR

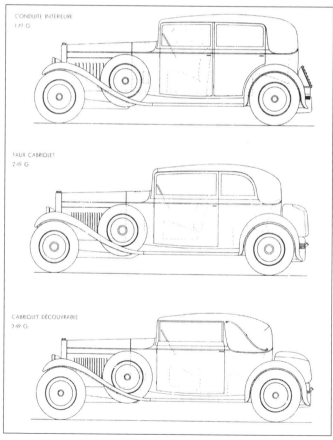

CONDUITE INTÉRIEURE 1.49 G

FAUX CABRIOLET 2.49 G

CABRIOLET DÉCOUVRABLE 3.49 G

A facsimile showing the Type 49 in the Gangloff catalogue.

Fac-similé d'un catalogue Gangloff pour le type 49.

An unusual wooden-decked touring car, but with later modifications to trunk and rear wing; chassis number 441010. Influenced by the similar style of the Renault 45 (Renault 40CV).

Chassis numéro 441010 avec un radiateur et un moteur de 49. Carrosserie pontée provenant d'une Renault 40CV.

Chassis number 49381 bodied by Pritchard-Demollin of Liège in Belgium. The American styling is evident; this car still exists.

Chassis numéro 49381 carrosserie pontée par Pritchard-Demollin de Liège. Influence américaine évidente; la voiture a été récemment très bien restaurée.

Chassis number 44746. Coachbuilder unknown. This car still survives.
Chassis numéro 44746. Carrossier inconnu. Voiture existante.

A well-executed new body on chassis number 49542.
Chassis numéro 49542 avec une carrosserie récente très bien réalisée.

CHAPTER TWENTY

GANGLOFF

The primary body subcontractor to Bugatti was Gangloff of Colmar, approximately 35 miles to the south of Molsheim and thus very convenient. The vast majority of independent coachbuilders in France were situated in Paris, a considerable distance from the Bugatti works. Ettore Bugatti started his own coachbuilding department in the 1920s, and we believe the first models to receive 'in house' bodies, apart from the racing cars, were the Grand Sports' on Types 40 and 43, whilst the Fiacres may have been amongst the earliest closed bodies built by the works.

Georges Gangloff, the proprietor of several body works in Switzerland, took over the old established carriage works of the Wiedeker Company in 1922. It is certain that Wiedeker received several orders for bodies from Bugatti prior to the 1914-18 war.

Gangloff gradually increased production of bodies for Bugatti, and in particular was responsible for drop-head coupés, generally to outlines supplied by Bugatti,

but we believe all the detail work was carried out by the Gangloff drawing office. Special orders and sample bodies were invariably the work of Gangloff.

The firm also built up a considerable business in bus and coach bodies, and this work continued after the 1939-45 war when private car coachwork orders had virtually ceased. Gangloff sold out to Lohr in 1993, and this company continued to use the Gangloff name until 1995.

Type 44, chassis number 441259, a Gangloff coupé. Note the distinctive Bugatti-style wing swaging.
Type 44 numéro 441259; coupé Gangloff avec une courbure d'ailes prononcée.

Type 44, chassis number 44608. This car was fitted with a torpedo body in October 1928; later the owner commissioned a new Gangloff coupé body to be fitted in 1935 in the Type 57 idiom. This car was fitted with twin electric petrol pumps, and the bonnet was provided with louvres; features installed because the owner lived in Val d'Isere and anticipated fuel and cooling problems due to altitude. The first owner had the car for fifty years.
Type 44 numéro 44608 Coupé Gangloff dans le style des 57. Remarquer les fentes sur le haut du capot pour améliorer le refroidissement, demandé par le premier propriétaire qui résidait à Val d'Isère et garda la voiture pendant 50 ans.

Another Gangloff coupé.
Autre coupé Gangloff.

Chassis number 49395 a standard drophead coupé by Gangloff. Note the untidy hood when furled.
Type 49 numéro 49395. Cabriolet par Gangloff. Remarquer la hauteur du toit une fois replié.

Type 49, chassis number 49244, another Gangloff coupé. Now at the Rochetaillée Museum.
Type 49 numéro 49244. Coupé Gangloff. Au musée de Rochetaillée.

Type 49, chassis number 49486, a Gangloff coupé, with a similar door and window line to the early Type 57 Stelvio.
Type 49 numéro 49486. Coupé Gangloff avec un dessin de portes et de vitres semblable aux premières 57 Stelvio.

A Gangloff coupé, probably 49402, exhibited at the Paris Salon in 1931.
'Véhicule exposé au Salon Automobile de Paris en 1931, sans doute 49402.

Another Gangloff with high-set headlamps, fabric top, and panelled below the waistline.
Une autre Gangloff, avec des phares montés haut, toit en simili-cuir et tôle sous la ligne de ceinture.

A unique and attractive drophead style coupé with leather top, the work of Gangloff and believed photographed in Colmar. Note the untidy cutout around the steering drop arm. Photographed when new in the winter of 1932-33.
Cabriolet avec toit en cuir, réalisé par Gangloff et sans doute photographié à Colmar, l'hiver de 1932-33.

Well known 1928 factory publicity shots of L'Ebé, Lydia and Roland with the catalogue Gangloff coupé styled by Bugatti. Note the peculiar air vents in the bonnet.
Publicité bien connue avec l'Ebé, Lydia et Roland d'un coupé sur un dessin de Bugatti réalisé par Gangloff. Remarquer les sorties d'air spéciales sur le capot.

A Type 44, chassis number unknown, but the coachbuilder is believed to be Gangloff.
Type 44 de numéro inconnu, sans doute carrossé par Gangloff.

Type 44 1929 production Gangloff saloon but with fully opening roof and garish patterned moquette upholstery.
Berline 44 Gangloff de 1929 à toit ouvrant avec un bel intérieur en tissu.

A late Gangloff Type 49, photographed circa 1950 but believed since scrapped.
Autre Gangloff de Type 49, photographié dans les années 50 mais sans doute détruit depuis.

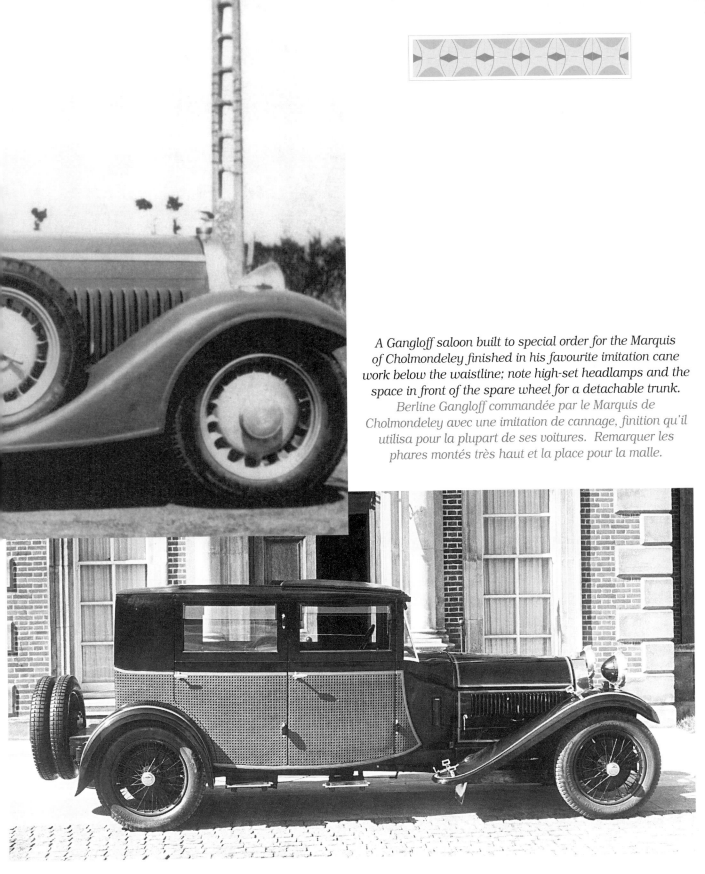

A Gangloff saloon built to special order for the Marquis of Cholmondeley finished in his favourite imitation cane work below the waistline; note high-set headlamps and the space in front of the spare wheel for a detachable trunk.
Berline Gangloff commandée par le Marquis de Cholmondeley avec une imitation de cannage, finition qu'il utilisa pour la plupart de ses voitures. Remarquer les phares montés très haut et la place pour la malle.

Gangloff saloon (Type 49) for Lord Cholmondeley, again with cane finish below the waistline and high-set headlamps. Registered in London in 1931.

Berline Gangloff (Type 49) de Lord Cholmondeley avec cannage et phares montés très haut. Immatriculée à Londres en 1931.

First series Gangloff saloon on the Type 49, chassis number 49294. This car still exists.

Berline 49 Gangloff de début de série; existe encore (chassis numéro 49294).

A pillarless Gangloff saloon dating from 1932, chassis number 49377.
Berline Gangloff de 1932 (chassis numéro 49377).

Chassis number 49255 a Gangloff saloon with different styling from standard. Note the heavily raked windscreen and opening quarter lights in the front doors. This car resides in Sweden.
Chassis numéro 49255, berline Gangloff d'un style inhabituel. Remarquer l'angle du pare-brise et les déflecteurs sur les portes avant. Voiture en Suède.

A long chassis limousine by Gangloff, believed to be the only example built and still in existence. Chassis number 49132, at the Paris Salon, 1930. Note the Perspex bonnet fitted for exhibition purposes.

Limousine de Gangloff, chassis long, numéro 49132. Exposée au Salon de l'Automobile de 1930 avec un capot en Plexiglas pour montrer le moteur.

Driver's compartment of chassis 49132. The steel steering wheel frame is entirely covered in walnut.

Intérieur de la voiture 49132. Les branches en acier du volant sont recouvertes de bois.

A 1932 Gangloff composite fabric and metal-bodied saloon photographed at the Molsheim Works. One can see Bugatti hinges on the factory door.

Carrosserie Gangloff de 1932. Berline avec toit en simili-cuir photographiée à Molsheim. Remarquer la porte de l'usine et ses charnières en bronze à l'arrière plan.

Chassis number 49510 by Gangloff.
Chassis numéro 49510, carrosserie Gangloff.

A well restored Gangloff body on chassis number 44881.
Chassis numéro 44881 avec une carrosserie Gangloff très bien restaurée.

Another Gangloff style, lower and more curvaceous, on chassis number 44375.
Chassis numéro 44375 avec une carrosserie Gangloff plus basse et aux courbes réussies.

Yet another Gangloff version with a foreshortened rear quarter panel. Chassis number 441144.
Autre Gangloff, chassis numéro 441144, pavillon de custode très étroit.

A Gangloff coupé inside a tobacconist shop; we believe staged for film work.
Coupé Gangloff dans un débit de tabac! on peut penser qu'il s'agit d'un film.

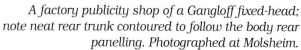

A factory publicity shop of a Gangloff fixed-head;
note neat rear trunk contoured to follow the body rear
panelling. Photographed at Molsheim.
*Carrosserie Gangloff; photo de publicité prise à
Molsheim. Faux cabriolet. Remarquer l'intégration de
la malle et de l'arrière de la carrosserie.*

An unusual Gangloff fixed-head, photographed on the
route de Saverne, a favourite venue for works publicity
shots. This car is possibly a Type 38.
*Un faux cabriolet Gangloff photographié sur la route de
Saverne, souvent utilisée pour les publicités de l'usine.
Cette voiture pourrait être un Type 38.*

An elegant faux cabriolet by Gangloff on an early Type 49; note the lowvred side valances and no running boards.
Un élégant faux cabriolet Gangloff de Type 49 début de série. Remarquer le capot, l'absence de marchepied et la malle amovible.

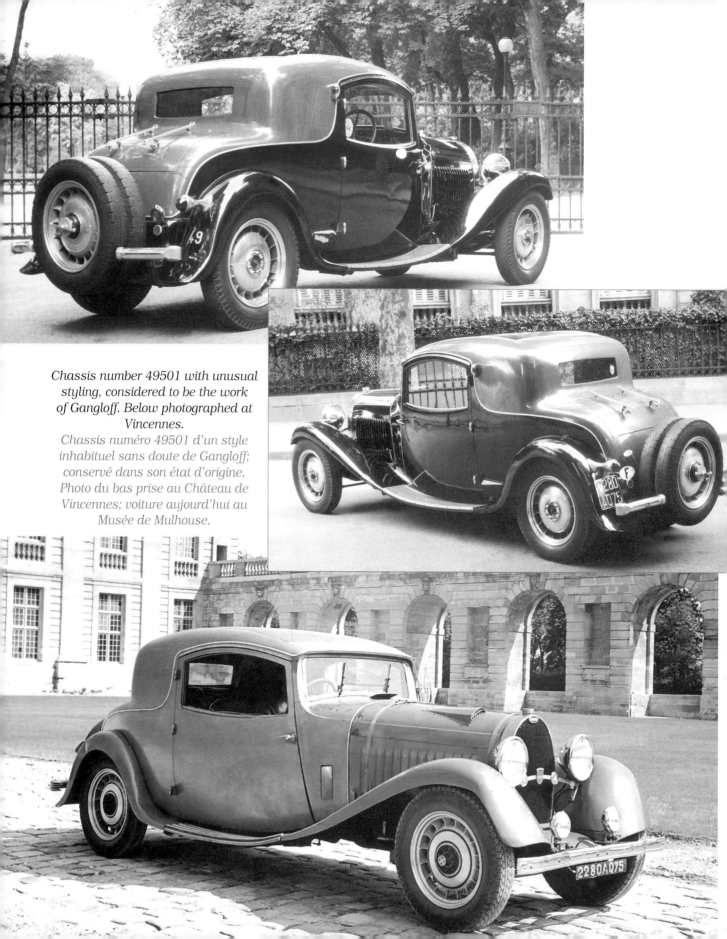

Chassis number 49501 with unusual styling, considered to be the work of Gangloff. Below photographed at Vincennes.

Chassis numéro 49501 d'un style inhabituel sans doute de Gangloff; conservé dans son état d'origine. Photo du bas prise au Château de Vincennes; voiture aujourd'hui au Musée de Mulhouse.

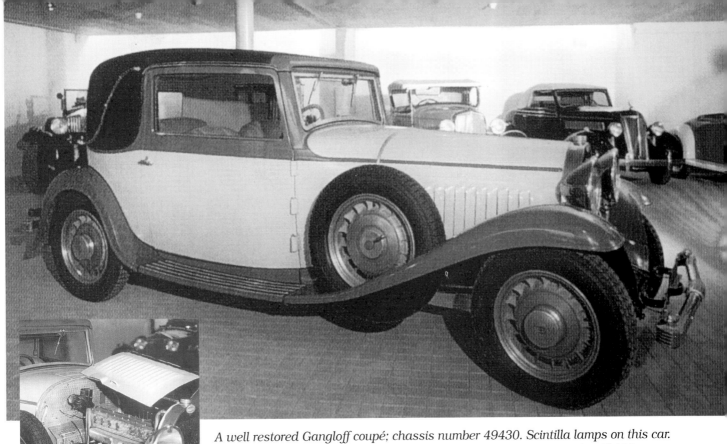

A well restored Gangloff coupé; chassis number 49430. Scintilla lamps on this car.
Coupé Gangloff bien restauré. Phares Scintilla-chassis numéro 49430.

A striking Type 49 believed to be Gangloff to special order; note the Fiacre scuttle effect and unusual valance treatment in the Art Deco idiom.
Type 49 sans doute de Gangloff; dessin très particulier de la porte rappelant la ligne Fiacre.

A sample Gangloff body on a late Type 49. Note the Art Deco door handle common to the later Type 57.
Carrosserie Gangloff sur un chassis de 49 de fin de série; remarquer la poignée de porte Art Déco semblable à celle d'une 57.

Chassis number 49385, a close-coupled coupé by Gangloff, with dickey seat and golf door.
Chassis numéro 49385. Coupé fermé de Gangloff avec siège dans le coffre et trappe pour clubs de golf.

Chassis number 49353, a well-restored surviving Gangloff.
Chassis numéro 49353. Carrosserie Gangloff bien restaurée.

An early Gangloff; note the enlarged rear window and pillarless construction on chassis number 44252.
Chassis numéro 44252. Gangloff de début de production. Remarquer la taille de la vitre arrière et construction sans montant central.

A standard 1931 pattern Type 49 Gangloff (49194), photographed in the early post-war years.
Type 49 par Gangloff (49194), carrosserie de leur catalogue, photographiée dans les années 50.

A similar car, with subtle changes from standard and unfortunate later attempts at 'modernisation'.
Une voiture semblable avec quelques modifications; il est regrettable qu'elle ait été modernisée.

Fixed head coupé by Gangloff, interior view (chassis number 49430).
Intérieur d'un faux cabriolet Gangloff. chassis 49430.

A late Gangloff, now in the Mulhouse Museum; chassis number 49545.
Chassis numéro 49545, carrossé par Gangloff. Au Musée de Mulhouse.

Early Type 49 (chassis number 49135) by Gangloff. This car still exists.
Voiture de debut de serie qui existe toujours. Numéro de chassis 49135.

Chassis number 49377, another special Gangloff saloon, but with trailing doors and aluminium mouldings around the door lights.
Chassis numéro 49377; berline Gangloff d'un modèle particulier avec portes à charnières avant et encadrements des fenêtres en aluminium.

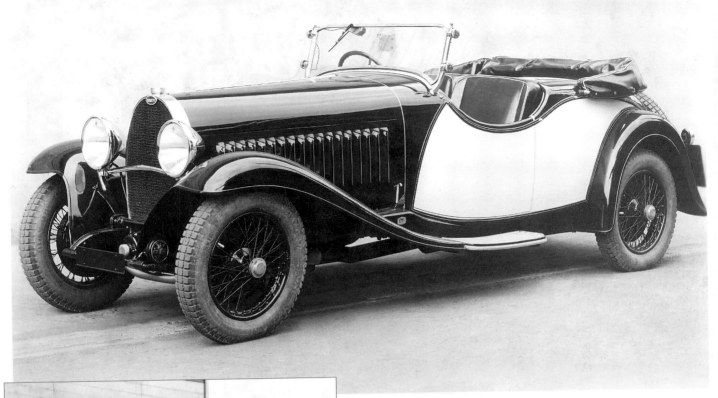

*Above and left: A special sample body by Gangloff on an
early Type 49, chassis number 49221.*
*Chassis numéro 49221, carrosserie spéciale de Gangloff
sur un Type 49 de début de série.*

*Below: The same car competing in the Paris-Nice Rallye,
June 1932. The car is now fitted with separate side lights
and front bumper.*
*La même voiture au Rallye Paris-Nice (juin 1932) avec feux
de position et pare-chocs.*

Type 49 (49431) with Gangloff roadster body; note the folding windscreen, in the manner of early Type 57 Stelvio coupés. Photo taken in 1958, at the Rallye du Mans.

Carrosserie Gangloff (49431) pour un roadster de Type 49; pare-brise repliable comme celui des premiers coupés 57 Stelvio. Photo prise en 1958 au Rallye du Mans.

The same car after restoration, aluminium wheels now fitted.
'La même voiture après restauration.

Type 38 with unusual 'all-weather' body by Gangloff and carriage-type door handles.
Type 38 par Gangloff ave une capote de grandes dimensions. Poignées de portes de type fiacre.

The Type 44 saloon, sober but elegant, as befitting a professional man with sporting pretensions, registered in the Limoges Préfecture of the Haut-Vienne department in August 1928. A note on the back of the original photograph declares it to be, 'My fifth Bugatti, 3 litres, 8 cylinders. Engine very flexible and quiet'. It also tells us that it completed a run from Vierzon to Limoges, 184km at an average of 90km/h. Coachbuilder, believed Gangloff, chassis number unknown.

Un Type 44 aux lignes suples élégantes, immatriculé en août 1928 à Limoges. Au dos de la photo, cette note, 'Ma cinquième Bugatti, une 3 litres, 8 cylindres-moteur suple et puissant'. J'ai fait 90 de moyenne sur les 184km du trajet Vierzon à Limoges. Carrosserie sans doute Gangloff, numéro de chassis inconnu.

BARRIE PRICE & JEAN LOUIS ARBEY

BUGATTI
TYPE 40

ISBN 978-1-901295-52-8 • £37.50*

BUGATTI 57
THE LAST FRENCH BUGATTI
– ENLARGED & REVISED EDITION –

BARRIE PRICE

ISBN 978-1-901295-66-5 • £35.00*

BARRIE PRICE

BUGATTI
TYPE 46 & 50
THE BIG BUGATTIS

ISBN 978-1-901295-69-6 • £29.99*

ARMSTRONG SIDDELEY MOTORS

The cars, the company and the people in definitive detail

BILL SMITH

ISBN 978-1-904788-36-2 • £75.00*

The Rise of **Jaguar**

A detailed study of the 'Standard era' 1928 to 1950

Barrie Price

ISBN 978-1-904788-27-0 • £37.50*

ROLLS-ROYCE
SILVER SPIRIT & SILVER SPUR
BENTLEY
MULSANNE, EIGHT, CONTINENTAL, BROOKLANDS & AZURE

MALCOLM BOBBITT

Updated & enlarged Second Edition

ISBN 978-1-904788-75-1 • £34.99*

Veloce Classic Reprint Series

BENTLEY MkVI

ROLLS-ROYCE Silver Wraith, Silver Dawn & Silver Cloud
BENTLEY R-Series & S-Series

Martyn Nutland

ISBN 978-1-845840-68-6 • £35.00*

158

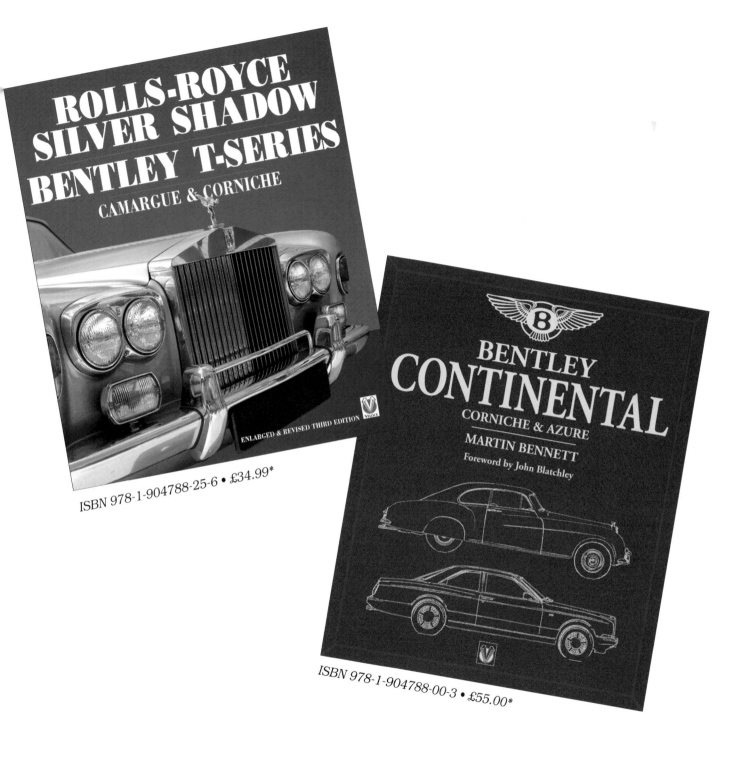

ISBN 978-1-904788-25-6 • £34.99*

ISBN 978-1-904788-00-3 • £55.00*

INDEX